DOGGY 'TAILS'
from East London

Published by the
East London Retired Dog Handlers

First published in 2009
by the East London Retired Dog Handlers

John Barrett
john@policegifts.co.uk

Printed by www.direct-pod.com Brixworth Northampton.

All profits from this book will go to
Care of Police Survivors (COPS)

Dedicated to all our long suffering wives and families and all those handlers no longer with us, not forgetting all those great dogs we miss so much.

Acknowledgements

We needed much help and advice to get this project into some shape and would like to thank a family member and friends who gave both.

Stewart Furness – a grandson who can use more than one finger on a computer and put up with the endless question "How?"

Chrissie & Alan Button – they took away all the worries as we got to the end and did not know what to do next
www.thebuttons.co.uk

John and Kevin at the Coppermill Press –
as always great service

John Edwards (JEDD) who has once again shown his unique talent with his great images for this book

Fred & Heather Feather for proof reading

Published by the East London Retired Dog Handlers

Distributed by Police gifts.
john@policegifts.co.uk

FOREWORD

By TONY JUDGE

(aka "Dogberry" in Police Magazine from 1968 to 1990)

Police dog handlers are, if they will forgive the description, a singular breed. They are, after all, equal partners of their canine comrades and it is the almost uncanny understanding that develops between the two that lies at the heart of their successes.

We are, broadly speaking, a nation of animal lovers, especially dogs, and although today the once universal good relations between police officers and law abiding citizens appear to be not what once they were, there can be no doubt that Joe Public still admires the police dogs for their courage and devotion to duty. Could this be because the dogs represent the best example of what people expect of their police - no nonsense gimmicks and irritating political correctness, just determination to maintain the law and bring villains to book?

Whilst the dogs and their handlers engaged themselves in the serious matters to be dealt with in the metropolis, this is a peep into the lighter side of their work and the characters of both the dogs and humans and demonstrates the underlying sense of humour which is vital for the discharge of their duties. No heroics here, just humour. It is therefore fitting that the proceeds are going to support the COPS charity, to benefit a group of men and women who have demonstrated that they too have shown the same courage in the service of the public.

Contents

Introduction

Producing this collection of dogs' tails (alright, tales!) has been a pure labour of love for everyone involved. It is our honest belief that all our readers will quickly see why it has been such a pleasure putting it together.

The stories are true accounts of things that actually happened. Well, they started as true stories, but we all know how policemen's tales improve with every telling across the canteen table or the bar of the "Crown & Horses".

They reflect a time when the business of policing and the attitude of those who did it were different from what goes on today. The stories cover the years from the 1950s to the 1980s, and it is a fact that many of the events you will read about, while not unusual in their day, could not be contemplated in today's climate of targets, strict conformity and (worst of all) political correctness.

In the period covered within these pages there was room for individuality and for personalities. Every parade room saw them at the start of every shift – but now, of course, there are no pre-shift parades and certainly little room for characterful coppers!

Inside these pages you'll find the memoirs of ordinary officers who went about their duties in just one of the Met's dog sections, but they reflect what went on in other parts of the Metropolitan Police as well as all the other forces throughout Britain.

Several threads bind them all together. The lads were all coppers of course and they all worked with dogs, but on top of that is the fact that in those days you had to be a special kind of copper to become a dog man.

And if you are or have been a dog handler you may well see yourself in our pages, even if you were hundreds of miles away at the time.

Let's hear it for the dogs and their handlers!

No 3 DISTRICT OF THE METROPOLITAN POLICE

The old No 3 District of the Metropolitan Police covered the northeast area of London, policed by 'E', 'G', 'H', 'J', and 'K' Divisions, which, apart from E Division, took in all of East London and the East End. There has always been some doubt, particularly in modern times, in the minds of many, where the geographical location of the 'East End' is. Any true East Ender will be in no doubt and tell you that it encompasses that area known as Tower Hamlets, after the old villages originally in the shadow of the Tower of London and bounded by the City of London in the west at Aldgate; the River Lea at Bow Bridge in the east, Victoria Park Road (South Hackney) to the north, along the northern foreshore of the River Thames east of Bow Creek. The whole area teems with history from the Vikings, Romans and Huguenots, through the mediaeval period and the more modern influxes of migrations from Ireland when the docks were built, Jews from Eastern Europe fleeing the Russian Pogroms and, even more recently, from Asia. The advents of WW1 & WW2 saw the area suffer from Zeppelin and Gotha bombers during WW1 and of course, the Blitz of WW2, followed by the aerial bombardment by the V1 flying bombs and V2 Rockets, wiping out large areas. 'H' Division was responsible for policing the East End with 'G' Division policing that area adjacent to the City of London Police along by Commercial Street.

The East End, always considered one of the roughest, toughest areas of London, featured in films and literature and more recently in the TV soap 'EastEnders', which is a parody of its people, who in no way resemble the miserable, thuggish bunch of 'chancers' portrayed. Once you got to know them and gained their respect, the true East Ender was a cheerful, good humoured, big hearted, genuine human being. It had its fair share of villains and unsavoury characters but no more than any other poor working class area of London. With history oozing from every brick, plus its people, policing the east of London and the East End could never be described as dull or boring – definitely not boring!

The day Frank Dew got annoyed

By RODNEY CROWHURST

I was a young officer who had just joined the section with Police Dog 'Widgery'. Roy Beale was our instructor at the district training ground – Chigwell. One cold winter morning and he wanted us to do crowd control practice, pushing back an unruly mob using the dog. It came to my turn and there in front of us were several handlers, shouting and yelling and playing the part of a crowd of unruly miscreants. Among them was the 'legend' known as Frank Dew, who never minced his words and was renowned for his forthright approach to the world!

Obeying instructions, I started to push the 'mob' back, with the dog barking and snapping at them. Frank was waving his arms about and making threatening gestures at my dog. I think he was cold and a little slow moving when the dog lunged forward and I then realised that the dog had stopped barking and was chewing something. He had half of a black leather glove in his mouth. The air turned from cold to 'blue' with a stream of invectives and expletives, calling doubt upon my ancestry!

It transpired Frank had been to the stores and issued with a new pair of gloves the day before. Need I say more? The exercise collapsed into total laughter.

Following this the exercise was promptly abandoned for a tea break. Yes it cost me a new pair of gloves for Frank ... please forgive me mate.

News of the incident soon circulated around the dog section. Roy Beale said it was the fastest he had ever seen Frank move, which caused more abuse and laughter.

The legend that was Ernie

By DENNIS WALLAND

Dave Ryan, having just come into the dog section, and Ernie Baxter were posted night duty to an observation in Central Park, East Ham. It was during winter and was cold, wet and quite miserable. They were posted one at each end of the park and were looking for a burglar who was thought to have crossed the park on his nefarious way to work. At one end of the park was a pavilion with a veranda, which afforded some, but not a lot of protection from the elements. At the other end was a small and slightly warmer hut in which to sit.

To make things fair and comparatively equal, they swapped each night, so that they each had to suffer the windswept discomfort of the open veranda every other night. Those who knew him would not be surprised to hear that on Ernie's night to sit on the veranda he arrived with a garden chair, a blanket, vacuum flask and his sandwiches, together with police dog 'Tiger'.

During the night Dave Ryan heard a bang, the crash of breaking glass and Ernie shouting. Thinking that Ernie had found the suspect, Dave ran to the pavilion, full of expectation.

Ernie had settled himself down with his blanket and chair and tied 'Tiger' to the leg of the chair with his tracking lead. He may, or may not, have been asleep (opinions differ on this point) when a cat walked past, presumably waking 'Tiger'. A bark and the cat made off, with 'Tiger' in hot pursuit. When 'Tiger' reached the end of the tracking lead the deck chair joined the chase tossing Ernie to the ground. The cat made off over a fence and across some allotments followed by Tiger, followed by the chair some distance behind, thus the crashing sound of glass when the chair met the cold frames on the allotments. Some distance behind all this was Ernie, still wrapped in his blanket calling in his sweet dulcet voice, "Tiigeeerrrr".

No burglars were caught that night but weren't we all lucky to have known the legend who was Ernie?

Norman & the Ladies

By NORMAN STEWART

I was late turn on the dog van with Taff Jones when we received a call to a block of flats on 'K' Division. Two dogs had gone berserk. On our arrival I saw 'K' Division station van, but no officers in sight. The informant pointed out a scruffy mutt and said "That's one, the other one is upstairs. They have just torn a cat to pieces".

I put a lead on the one she had pointed out, took it to the station van and put it into the back. That caused the two officers in the van to jump out of the front.

I took the dog catcher and went after the second one that was on a second floor landing. It was cowering in a corner. I caught its head in the noose of the catcher, and then realised I would have to walk backwards to get down to ground level. I called over the landing wall to a young P.C from 'K' to give me a hand. When he came up I said to him "I've got the end that bites, you put your hand under its tail and grab its balls and squeeze hard, I won't let go of this end".

Slowly we made our way to the van and thence to the station. When we got to the station it was then I discovered that both of the dogs were bitches. To this day I have no idea what it was that the young PC was holding.

'Tails' from the crypt

By BOB MARRION

Arriving at Bow police station for a late, late shift covering the late evening and night hours, I was told to go home, get a civilian jacket, some sandwiches and a thermos (I was living on the manor at the time), return to the station and present myself with dog to the CID. "Oh, good" I thought, "I am being taken on a picnic." This after a fashion I was, along with a grizzled, worldly wise, pre-war Scots CID officer who, I presumed wished for me and the dog to hold his hand while keeping observation in Tower Hamlets Cemetery.

It transpired that a member of staff had found a crypt open, which upon investigation had shown an amount of 'bluey'(lead) had been stripped and ready to remove. It was reasoned that the haul was going to be collected at the first opportunity.

After World War 2 Tower Hamlets Cemetery was very overgrown, but peaceful enough to walk around on a nice summer's day, and a picnic among the graves and tombs seemed very much in order. With the sun setting and the last vestiges of daylight fading into twilight, we moved down into the vault, hiding in a spot previously reconnoitred and agreed upon amongst the various coffins, etc.

Preparing ourselves for a possibly long and unrewarding vigil, our wait was not too long before voices were heard from above and a torchlight beam cut through the gloom, accompanied by descending footsteps. The light from the torch revealed one suspect, with probably the others waiting at the exit of the crypt at the top of the stairs. Our villain, fully occupied in man handling his heavy burden of sheet lead, had his back towards us and did not hear my erstwhile CID colleague carefully creep from his hiding place. Placing his hand on the unsuspecting villains shoulder along with the word, "Gotcha", the suspect collapsed without a sound, no shriek of terror, any orgasmic moan, just silent collapse!

By this time the dog could hardly control himself, having been held under restraint and on command launched himself up the stairs. The sight of what must have appeared a hound from hell, or a reincarnation of the Hound of the Baskervilles, hurling itself out of the darkness of the crypt had a most chastening effect on the second suspect who was rooted to the spot. With hair standing on end and eyes like chapel hat pegs, I left the dog to guard the prisoner – he obviously was not going anywhere with a large, highly excited animal whose slavering jaws were about an inch from his crotch – and I returned down into the Stygian darkness to see what was happening to our other grave robber, who was just about recovering and being hauled into an upright position. "Bloody Hell, Jock (at the time the 'thought police' was only operating in Eastern Europe and it was nothing unusual or out of order to call colleagues: 'Jock', 'Taff', 'Paddy', 'Dusty', 'Chalky', 'Ginger', etc., without any offence being given, or taken), I thought you had killed him." "Well, laddie", he replied," I couldn't have chosen a better place for it to have happened if I had!"

With that imparted bit of wisdom, we walked our prisoners towards the 'nick' as the accompanying accumulated odour of evacuated bowels was deemed too strong for the enclosed space of the general purpose van. Anyway, it was a nice night for a stroll!

"Message Received – will be there tomorrow!"
Photograph of unknown origin, showing a Morgan car in 1929

The legend that was Frank Peters & Fred

By JOHN BARRETT

Frank Peters and his dog Fred had one thing in common, they both shared a 'Short Fuse'. Frank was a stocky, medium height man who wore glasses.

Those of us who knew Frank were wise enough to know that if he took his glasses off, folded them up and put them away, someone was going to get hurt.

I remember one night duty at about 2am, sitting on a wall together with a night duty emergency doctor while Frank and the doctor's driver had a coming together about the other's driving.

The Doctor said to me, "Is your driver always like this?" I said, "Yes he is". The doctor replied, "So is mine".

After a few minutes, with no injuries but pride restored, we both went about our separate duties.

We were once doing a search in a garage storage yard, full of cars waiting to be sold. My dog "Zola" had found a suspect and was barking. Fred had also found the second one but was eating him... These were a pair well matched and confirm the theory "It goes down the lead or even it goes up the lead" Great to work with both Frank and Fred and no day was ever dull.

The best or the worst

By DENNIS WALLAND

Being stationed at Romford police station it was my custom, when on foot patrol, to leave the station by way of the rear door, walk along the back of the Magistrates' Court, then through the court car park and out onto Main Road and thence into town.

Midway along this route was a five feet wall and on the other side was a small park, which at some time in the past had been a cemetery of some kind. Among the few gravestones there was an area of grass which was much appreciated by my dog, 'Nimbus', as a place to get rid of any waste products his body had to offer, before assuming the more dignified appearance expected of a police dog. Nimbus would scale the wall and indulge himself while I would walk on and wait for him to catch me up at Main Road.

Many times we had gone through this routine but one particular Sunday evening it was different.

Everything I have described so far happened as usual, but as I waited at the Main Road I realised that 'Nimbus' was taking longer than usual. Then, from out of the darkness, I heard a horrific scream. It was truly awful. No dog barking so I had no idea what was happening. I ran back and looked over the wall. The screaming got louder and was now hysterical. I shone my torch there and saw a strange sight, which took a little while for me to assimilate.

He was lying on his back, she was astride him, there was not a stitch of clothing between them, and it had all been put in a very neat pile beside them. Her hair was long and hung down over his face. Her body was what could be called voluptuous, her bottom was well rounded and there with his nose pressed against this comely bum was 'Nimbus'. I'm not sure if he was sniffing or licking but certainly he was interested in this rare opportunity to exercise his olfactory senses, apparently oblivious to her wild sobbing screams.

I did the decent thing and after carefully illuminating the scene with my torch (which on this rare and wonderful occasion actually worked) I called my dog and left. I then stood in a dark doorway and watched this pair of lovers, hurriedly attired and she still sobbing hysterically, scuttling, and I really mean scuttling, past.

Looking back, I sometimes wonder, was this the best or worst he ever had, I'm pretty certain I know what she would have thought of it.

Anyone for 'Chase the Lady'?

By BOB MARRION

One of the more serious outbreaks of public disorder in the Metropolitan Police District after World War 2 was what is now known as the Notting Hill Race Riots. The hierarchy feared that, like ripples on a still pond, disturbances would break out wherever there was a black or more cosmopolitan populace, or in areas where they tended to congregate.

Such a location was Cable Street, on Leman Street's patch. Always a tough area going back many, many years when one of its adjacent streets, Radcliffe Highway (now known as The Highway) was one of the worst villainous 'stews' in London and believed to be the setting for Charles Dickens' Fagin's Den in 'Oliver Twist.' Cable Street will also be remembered for the pitched battle between Oswald Moseley's Blackshirts and many of the Jewish population who lived in the area prior to the outbreak of WW2. An area very close to the River Thames, it was a haven for many denizens of the night, full of seedy cafes, brothels and illegal gaming houses enlivened by the whiff of burning camel dung associated with the smoking of 'wacky baccy'.

To nip in the bud any potential increase in hostilities, weekends usually being a battleground anyway and normally good for a quick four hours overtime at Thames Magistrates Court, it was decided to increase police presence with the 'H' & 'G' division dog handlers descending en masse during the hours of darkness and early morning, either patrolling the area, or being kept on reserve at Leman Street.

Police stations at that time were not equipped to kennel police dogs, a kennel for strays being the only available accommodation for canines and highly unsuitable for our charges, for obvious reasons. So police dogs usually accompanied us into the canteen and were generally welcomed and accepted by all.

One particular night which, for a change, was proving to be a rather quiet one, all four 'H' division dogs were on reserve and in the canteen. As was the practise, leads were looped or tied either around a table leg or chair leg while the respective handlers, Don Edwards with 'Prince', Fred Collins with 'Lucky III', John MacDonald with 'Nero' plus myself with 'Lucky IV', all sitting at the same table enjoying refreshment (whatever would we have done without egg, sausage and chips!?) while also participating in a friendly game of 'Chase the Lady' or 'Hearts'.

Now, a week or so of attachment to Leman Street had taught the dogs to recognise the system of bell signals for transport, should drivers be in the canteen, i.e. one bell for the General Purpose car driver, two bells for the van driver and three bells for the 's**t has hit the fan, all hands to the pump'.

At one bell the dogs normally just opened one eye; at two bells, both eyes were opened and ears cocked, at three bells, they were up, rearing to go and straining at the leash! On this occasion if my memory serves me correctly, two of the dogs were tied to one table, one to the next and another to the chair leg where the particular handler was seated, when the three bells sounded. The ensuing chaos of two tables, one chair with their canine appendages, four handlers trying to free their charges, plus assorted other bodies being jammed in the canteen doorway, slipping and sliding through the remains of a variety of beans, eggs, sausages and chips, nicely mixed with brews of tea or coffee, was reminiscent of a Max Sennet Keystone Cops comedy episode!

The first to free itself from the ruck was 'Lucky III', who, with the van driver, was in the van awaiting the eager posse of handlers and foot police who, once loaded and in a variety of stages of dress or undress, headed off towards the scene of the occurrence; hazy recollection believes this to have been one of the seedy side streets leading to Cable Street.

On arrival it was found that we had left Fred Collins, 'Lucky III's' handler behind, not that this seemed to matter to the dog who performed magnificently by remote control prior to Fred arriving huffing and puffing a little later and probably breaking some kind of track record for sprinting the half mile or so from the 'nick'. Happy days!

The Leman Street Strutter's Ball

By BOB MARRION

Warm summer evenings, particularly on a Friday or Saturday, usually meant a busy tour of duty for us of the inner 'fish and chip' divisions of 'H' and 'G'. Patrolling in one of the old converted transit dog vans with Frank Gavin and 'Bruce', plus a driver from Leman Street police station, it was not too long into a night duty before a call went out for urgent assistance required at the 'Prospect of Whitby' Public House, Wapping. The 'Prospect' was not the normal kind of watering hole frequented by the ordinary citizens of the area, it being more of an attraction to drinkers from further afield, including overseas visitors because of its historical background and the chance of seeing someone 'famous', which at times happened.

We were soon on scene, greeted by the sight of a heaving mass of humanity spilling out of the pub onto the pavement and roadway, all valiantly trying to be controlled by two hard pressed PC's, who were obviously fighting a losing battle – literally! One particular section of the throng appeared to be more obstreperous and excited than the rest, who were quite bad enough, Worst of all, a glint of metal was perceived to be waved round. Frank and I immediately went into action separating this noisy faction from the remainder. After numerous requests of 'Please gentleman, depart from this place forthwith and forever hold your peace,' followed by the more normal mode of address to miscreants of the highways and byways of East London, i.e. "P*** off or get knocked off." They didn't, and they were! Still seemingly unable to do anything that they were told, complete with musical instruments (which was the glint of metal seen by us), the whole ensemble was ferried by various means to Leman Street police station where, on being deposited in the charge room, they were still highly irate and protesting in a foreign language.

Leman Street was always guaranteed to be busy, but at weekends it was more so and in no way could be considered a haven of rest, from the time the pubs turned out until those habituates of the wee small hours tottered off to their 'flops'. The original Leman Street Police Station was constructed with cells on two floors, the upper floor generally reserved for female prisoners. At weekends, however, when cell accommodation throughout the division tended to get a little scarce, overloads from the other stations were farmed out to Leman Street, if there was any room left.

So, picture if you can, a charge room already crammed with assorted vomiting drunks, prostitutes of all shapes and sizes waving their knickers in the air (if they were wearing any), among other things, plus a sprinkling of other ne'er do wells, much expanded by the introduction of a large number of excitable, musical instrument waving individuals. Bedlam reigned! Few of our noisy mob could string two intelligible words of English together, and foreign language to any degree of fluency was not our remit, other than some Yiddish (to the uninitiated, a vernacular form of Hebrew) which at times could prove useful in the East End.

The Station Officer was pre-WW2, police and WW2 ex-armed services, a both wily and unflappable character who decided that any action must come from one who is paid to make such decisions. So the Duty Officer was sent for. In the interim, the musicians' English minder had made an appearance, he having been separated from his charges during the melee at the 'Prospect' and eased the situation considerably, our musicians now being identified as a Dutch student jazz band in this country on a goodwill or exchange visit (Oops!).

Again we were fortunate in the calibre of Duty Officer, he also being another pre-war and ex-WW2 type imbued with his fair share of common sense – something that appears to be sadly lacking today. Both he and the Station Officer went into a huddle, finally deciding on an action lessening the likelihood of a diplomatic incident. As no police officer had been crowned by a trumpet or clarinet; there having been no malicious or wilful damage done, with no complaints forthcoming from the publican or members of the public, and wishing to relieve the press of bodies in the charge room, now bursting at the seams, the whole resembling something of a scene of an illustration by Hogarth, the band was released without charge. Two conditions (unofficial) were attached and explained to them through their interpreter and minder, the first that an impromptu performance should be given.

Coppers being ever the cynics that they are, started to drift towards the street eager to be out of the overloaded and rather 'ripe' atmosphere of raucous drunks and brazen 'brasses' when the band started up. It became very obvious that these boys were certainly not what one could term 'amateurs' – they were good. In a short space of time the 'nick' was rocking to a selection of good classic trad' jazz, 'Wolverine Blues', 'Kansas City Stomp', 'The Woodchoppers Ball' etc. It wasn't long before a PC and WPC were 'cutting a rug' on the charge room table, with a virtuoso performance of the 'Jitterbug', to a highly appreciative audience of coppers and denizens of the night, all stamping their feet and clapping their hands to the music. The music was so good that passers by thought that Leman Street police station had converted to a jazz club and started to congregate outside. That night, music certainly did tame the savage breast, as it was not every night it could be said the Metropolitan Police provided high class entertainment for the long suffering constabulary, prisoners and the general public – not forgetting the Dutch, of course!

Calm finally being restored, prisoners smilingly being led away to their cells and the Dutch jazz band heading off into the early dawn, a modicum of normality settled on Leman Street. Oh yes! The second 'condition' was that the band should return next morning and take up position beneath the Chief Superintendent's window overlooking Leman Street and they perform for him. We said that we felt he would appreciate it. I wonder if they did. We never did ascertain what caused the original fracas.

As no stretch of the imagination in today's litigious society would anything truly vaguely resembling the above happen, where the 'sharks' of the legal profession are forever seeking reasons for people to claim COM-PEN-SAY-SHUN. This goes a long way in explaining the po-faced and politically correct police we now have.

Wives' tales

By PAM VENABLES

Before Dog: Pat, my husband had just left Peel House police training college and we moved into our flat at Walthamstow. The kitchen was really awful so we decided to redecorate it. Pat knew absolutely nothing about DIY and decorating but undeterred we bought new cabinets etc and full of anticipation we set about the task at about 6pm one Saturday.

Full of enthusiasm, Pat hammered away and put a nail through a water pipe. In those days we didn't have a phone of our own so off he went to the phone box at the end of the road to phone for a plumber, leaving me standing on a chair, finger on the hole, like a small Dutch boy stopping a leaky dam.

On the way to the phone box, his pals in a police car pulled alongside Pat and shouted "got a call to Trafalgar Square, want to come?" Without a second thought Pat jumped in and off they went.

Hours went by, me still on the chair shifting first one arm then another. 10pm Pat appears flushed with excitement, "Where is the plumber?' says I. "What plumber is that then?" he replied. My next sentence is not suitable for publication in this book.

After Dog: Saturday night once again, Pat was on duty with police dog 'Gila'. For some reason which I never questioned, Pat and 'Gila' were chasing a man across a field.

When I tell you that 'Gila' had more sense than Pat you may understand why the dog ran around the slurry pit whilst Pat went in it right up to his neck.

I became aware of this when at about 10pm there was a ring at the front door and there stood Pat, soaking wet, not smelling of roses and feeling very sorry for himself. For the sake of decency I turned off the hallway light before getting a sack for him to stand on while I insisted he strip off every stitch of clothing before coming into my nice clean house.

For several days I avoided the neighbours in case anyone had seen this debacle and thereby avoided their awkward questions.

It's a dog's life

By HARRY FELL

In the late '60's, on duty with John Barrett, on Juliet Zero dog van. The pubs were turning out at 10.30 pm as we were driving along High Road Leytonstone, John behind the wheel.

We saw half a dozen Herberts chasing one bloke. We drove on and stopped at the Halfway House pub, facing the way from which the Herberts were coming. The party came up to us and we allowed the pursued to go, but we each grabbed two of the pursuers, nicking them for threatening behaviour. At that moment the Halfway House Pub emptied out onto the footway and a chap tapped one of my prisoners on the shoulder and said 'Have it on your toes, there is enough of us to take care of these two 'coppers.' We were being pushed and shoved by the crowd and suddenly there was an almighty roar and people backed away, leaving us a large space containing the mouthy git, and our prisoners with the dog van parked against the curb.

It would appear the situation was getting out of control. John managed to reach over and open the van door and released my dog 'Saul.' John knowing 'Saul' decided it was time to get out of the way and backed into a doorway. The mouthy git said to 'Saul' "Do you want a fight then?" and commenced to try and kick the dog. Anyone who remembers 'Saul' will know he excelled and relished this form of play, gleefully evading the kicks and whole heartedly entering into the spirit of the game, biting our recalcitrant 'nosy parker' on any part of his anatomy in easy reach of his teeth. At the same time, he systematically stripped him of every stitch of clothing down to his vest, briefs, socks and shoes. I was obliged to let my two prisoners go and try and contain 'Saul'. By now, 'Saul' was in such a state of excitement, he started to include me amongst the ranks of the enemy, tearing my uniform jacket. Fortunately, our mouthy interloper had decided that enough was enough and had surrendered. At last I was able to get 'Saul' under some control but not before letting my two original prisoners go.

The GP van arrived, driven by Lew Turner and accompanied by the Duty Officer Inspector Jimmy Dickinson. I told both of them to watch our semi naked prisoner as I was not convinced that he was going to come quietly, which he didn't, kicking Lew Turner in the leg, following up with a 'Haymaker' punch which missed Lew as the force of the kick made him double up. The punch intended, missed Lew and hit Inspector Dickinson in the eye. He unwisely was standing immediately behind Lew.

At Stratford Magistrates Court the next morning I told the sad tale of the assault on the two police officers but all the bench wanted to know was that the police dog was alright and was not injured in anyway. They hadn't met 'Saul!'

Humpty Dumpty
By OLIVE MARRION

The thing that most, if not all, police wives dread, is the knock at the door in the dead of night, with police officers and a police vehicle standing outside the door. Such an occasion once happened to me. The feeling in the pit of my stomach and my sense of nausea was enhanced when I saw my husband's dog, 'Lucky', being held on a lead by another handler. Fearing the worst, my fears were soon allayed when I opened the street door to have them all burst into laughter, informing me that Bob was in Poplar Hospital after a high wall had collapsed under him and the prisoner, and they were holding hands in an A & E ward, glaring and cursing at one another. Before handing me the dog, the lads asked me to inform them, should he be detained, as they would pay him a visit and share his grapes! Fortunately, he wasn't, but suffered a badly damaged leg, doing everything but breaking it.

Lessons

By DENNIS WALLAND

I learned some very important lessons from Bill Bradfield. He was the dog handler at Ilford, long before I got into the section and I became his groupie. I followed him about all the time, eager to pick his brains, so that I could follow my dream and get a dog of my own. Night duty was the best because, after midnight, hardly anybody moved in those days, so we could relax a bit and I badgered him to show me his dog working.

He fixed me up with some padding and we gave his dog a bit of street training. The chase was Bill's favourite and so we set up a couple of scenarios.

I would run towards a petrol station at Seven Kings and he would send his dog to catch me. The well thought out plan was that I would jump on top of a petrol pump, so the dog would not be able to reach me, but would circle and bark.

Shell (the petrol company) boasted that their petrol contained ICA (Inner Cylinder Additive) and this was demonstrated by a seashell shaped illuminated sign, which was to be found on top of their petrol pumps.

That is when I learned my first lesson:
The ICA sign was not a secure fixing.

I ran, Bill shouted, the dog barked and then came after me like a runaway train. I jumped up on top of the petrol pump, grabbed hold of the ICA sign as I continued in my original trajectory, straight over the top. I lay on my back gripping a shell shaped ICA sign, with an angry dog securely fixed on my left leg.

Second Lesson: Dog bites hurt!

Not to be put off, we then hatched a really clever plan. This time I would run away in the direction of a telephone box. Before the dog reached me I would enter the box, close the door and be safe.

Third Lesson: Telephone boxes are equipped with a very clever spring which will prevent the door closing on you quickly, causing injury. Likewise, they do not take kindly to being pulled closed and will resist every effort to shut the door hurriedly, even when there is a raving police dog after you.

Fourth Lesson: As per lesson number two.

Thanks for all you taught me Bill Bradfield.

The Barbican

By JOE LANCASTER

One day in the 1960s I was on late turn duty in the dog van, in company with my best friend and colleague Bill (Harry) Sharp and his dog 'Flash', when we were called to a large block of offices in the Barbican. We were informed that there had been a breaking and it was believed that the suspect may still be on the premises.

Bill said he would search the ground and first floor, leaving me to search the third and top floors. In this way the dogs would not be distracted by each other. I searched the third floor thoroughly, with no indication from the dog of the presence of an intruder, so continued to the top floor where 'Silas' became agitated. We were in a long corridor with just a couple of offices which we searched and found to be empty. There was one door at the far end of the corridor, but again that office was clear. 'Silas' refused to leave a particular area of the corridor and was jumping up and attempted to climb the wall.

I looked up and found myself looking at the stars. There was a skylight in the ceiling, but it was much too high to climb to. By this time Bill had put his dog back in the van and decided to give me a hand. Bill was all of six foot four, and I suggested I climb onto his shoulders and maybe pull myself up. We both agreed that it was inconceivable that anyone could climb up a sheer wall to the skylight, but we decided to give it a try. Balanced precariously on Bill's shoulders I reached up, then gripping on the skylight frame pulled myself up. When my head reached the level of the skylight, I was looking into a pair of eyes, and this voice said "F*** me the man from Interpol".

He was lying along the edge of the roof and the skylight. Seeing the dog he was reluctant to climb down but I persuaded him that was the best option available to him. He then lowered himself through the skylight and dropped to the ground, while I struggled to get back down from Bill's shoulders. I asked the suspect how on earth he had managed to get up onto the roof from the corridor and his explanation was quite simple; He had a rope ladder from the roof and he had come down that, but would not disclose how he reached the roof of a four storey building. He had to be either Superman or Spiderman without the costume.

He stated, when arrested, that we had spent enough time finding him, and, had it not been for the dog, he would have got away with it. True! This was something he must have reflected on during his time in prison.

A quiet day out
By BOB MARRION

In times long past, it came to pass that those guardians of much of the earth's liquid gold, namely oil, decided that their main mode of transport, the camel, should be updated and replaced by gold plated Rolls Royces; also the telling of the time substituted by Rolex Oysters, rather than the position of the sun relative to the earth. To achieve this aim a demand was made for a greater share of the wealth generated by this asset. Tremors of shock and horror reverberated throughout Europe, ever reliant on oil since the advent of the internal combustion engine. Yes, it is said that even in AD117, the Roman 9th Hispanic Legion disappeared into the Pictish heartland mists, inhabited by the hairy kneed, oatmeal eating tribes, namely Caledonia, never to be seen again when it ran out of oil for its lamps.

I digress, however. The result of the intransigence by oil companies to cough-up extra revenue for crude oil led to supplies being radically reduced by the very 'miffed' sons of the desert, leading to the rationing of petrol.

In those early days, when police dogs were still a comparative novelty, each division transported its own dogs and handlers to their respective training grounds, No 3 District being situated at Chigwell Sports Club. The old station vans were used for this purpose. With usually no more than one or two dogs per trip for 'H' division, each division normally took care of its own, although occasionally a handler and dog from 'G' division was included.

The fuel crisis (as it became known) caused an order to be passed from those who had to be obeyed, who in their infinite wisdom, decreed that one station van, affectionately known by the local populace of the East End of London as the 'Black Maria' or 'Hurry Up Wagon', should be used for the transportation of handlers and their familiars from 'G', 'H' and 'K' Divisions. 'J' Division attended to its own, Chigwell being considered local. Under normal circumstances five dogs and their handlers could be accommodated comfortably and safely, if the front bucket seat was used. The new order tended to stretch things a little, dogs and handlers being unfamiliar to each other and a number being considered 'characters', which was considered the norm in the dog handling fraternity where, amongst some, the delights of early morning birdsong and beauties of daybreak were pure anathema. Suffice it to say, little imagination need be used to see the potential for some very interesting trips to the training ground.

One particular and unforgettable morning, an extra early start than normal was scheduled to pick up about nine dogs and handlers for conveyance to Chigwell. It was rather unfortunate that two dogs, 'Lucky 3' and 'Silas', stationed at that time at Bethnal Green and Bow respectively, had formed what can be best described as an antipathy towards each other, rarely neglecting the opportunity to get to grips if, and when, the opportunity presented itself, which it rarely did, both handlers being fully aware of the possibility of a rare old dog fight!

All dogs, at this time in the early dog programme, were gifts donated by the public, with a little 'uncertainty' as to their individual foibles and dispositions, plus the idiosyncrasies of a number of handlers themselves, added a certain 'piquancy' to dog handling. Nevertheless, if the dog had a leg at each corner, a good nose, a full set of 'choppers' matched with courage, they were deemed suitable for police work. Most were. The incumbent dog sergeant, recognisable not only by his three chevrons of rank but also by carrying a whip and a chair, had full knowledge of the tendencies between 'Lucky' and Silas'. He made sure that the former was picked up first and positioned next to the driver, with the handler seated on the bucket seat, while 'Silas' was boarded last of all to be as far away as possible in the rear of the van.

Fate, at times, deals some very cruel blows, and it came to pass that a certain van driver from Bow was detailed for this duty. To say that this particular driver was a little apprehensive of canines of all shapes, sizes and temperaments could be considered an understatement – he was petrified! Being a true stalwart and upholder of the brotherhood of the cloth, with orders being orders and thus to be obeyed, nerves were put aside. The handlers and their 'cherries' were duly collected in the order laid down, albeit with one cheek of the said driver's backside only being in position on his seat with the offside door left open (had it been possible to control the vehicle from outside- he would have done so), off we all set for Chigwell.

It must be said that with the arrival of 'Silas', the certain 'sixth sense' attributed to the animal world in general and dogs in particular became evident, the atmosphere becoming akin to the approach of a thunderstorm, the air seemingly charged with tension and menace, accompanied by low growls and rumblings from both dogs and handlers, the dogs being held firmly under restraint between the legs and arms of respective handlers, minimising the chance of a mishap. This still did not stop our two canine protagonists glaring balefully at each other from their respective positions.

It was towards the approach to Charlie Brown's Roundabout, after a seemingly uneventful journey that a slight lapse of concentration may have led to the loosening of restraining human appendages. The dogs by this time were becoming slightly restive at not being able to stretch out along the floor or bench seats, as was their custom normally. In the blink of an eye, or before you could say 'Pedigree Chum', 'Silas' was at 'Lucky' and in close combat. You could sense the rest of the dogs gleefully thinking 'punch up' and they, in turn, started to get stuck into the fray. If another dog wasn't available – human flesh would do!

By this time the van was negotiating the roundabout at Charlie Brown's. The driver, to his everlasting credit considering his almost pathological fear of the canine world, had been steering the vehicle hanging half in and half out of it, while gainfully controlling his bowels and looking forward to seeing the backs of his, by now, recalcitrant charges. His shredded nerves were finally broken when the fight between 'Lucky' and 'Silas' extended into the space housing the steering wheel and the driver's lap. With an anguished cry of either "Geronimo", or "S** this for a game of soldiers", the engine was stopped, handbrake applied and the intrepid driver bailed out and legged it to any haven of safety, free of kicking, cursing and punching handlers and ferociously scrapping dogs. Fortunately traffic was comparatively light, due to the aforesaid fuel crisis, plus traffic was not as heavy as we experience to-day, there also being an efficient and almost 24 hour public transport system.

It is quite surprising how quickly an enthusiastic crowd of onlookers formed to watch this mob of gladiatorial combatants (resembling a band of Balkan Banditti. No formal training attire was issued at that time, handlers wore an assemblage of 'informal' dress) doing credit to the Circus Maximus of the ancient Roman Coliseum. Eventually order was restored, the erstwhile driver retrieved from his nearby arboreal sanctuary and all eventually reaching our intended destination, bloodied, battered, with one, yet to be diagnosed broken wrist (the effects of which in the twilight of my years, I am suffering to this day!). Copious cups of hot sweet tea, coffee and rounds of toast eventually mollified a severely traumatised driver, who thankfully, after examining his various 'parts' for signs of irreparable damage, returned to Bow. I often wonder, however, why he never returned to pick us up for the return journey!

He was only trying to help

By NORMAN MASON

In the late 70's when I was a dog sergeant, I was supervising street training one evening in Ollerton Road, Islington. Street training is when we give the dogs experience in practical exercises in the area where they are employed.

I was suitably padded on my right arm and was practicing the chase for Norman Stuart and his dog Mirriam. I was running along the road and Norman instructed his dog to chase and stop me. Just as the dog was released a man came out from one of the houses and said "in here mate, I'll hold the copper". I thought good luck to you, if you can hold big Norman Stuart, all 6ft 6 inches of him, never mind the problem he was about to experience from 'Mirriam'. I politely declined his offer and our good Samaritan retained his liberty, unaware of how close he had come to an evening as a guest at Islington police station.

Late 1950's, I had just come from the dog school as a new dog handler and was on night duty at Wood Green police station. About 1am a call came for a dog to assist at Temple Fortune on S Division at the scene of a shop breaking.

I duly arrived at the scene with my dog 'Denver'. I put the tracking harness and line on the dog and cast the dog at the rear of the shop searching for a scent at the place where the suspects had last been seen.

Whilst the dog was casting for a track, a PC said "Here you are mate, give the dog a sniff of this, the suspects have had a go at it" and he held out a rather large meat pie. Naturally the dog wanted no encouragement and duly dispatched the evidence and thereafter had no wish to work anymore.

The dog then had a wee on the rear fence and decided it was time to go back to Wood Green having decided this police dog work was quite rewarding

Claybury Hospital (football crazy)

By JOHN BARRETT

Built between 1889 and 1893, Claybury Hospital was purpose built as a lunatic asylum, designed by George Thomas Hine on the site of an historic garden laid out in 1789, consisting of 50 acres of woodland and 95 acres of open parkland. Claybury could hold 2500 inmates and also was furnished with criminal detention wards. The old Victorian building was situated in vast grounds and at one time had its own orchards and many out buildings. Many parts of the grounds were overgrown.

As a result of a number of incidents of Police being called to search for 'missing' inmates, permission was given for 'J' division dog handlers to occasionally use the grounds for training purposes. When called out for a genuine search we were given a printed layout of the grounds, with descriptions of anything that would help with locating the missing person in this very large area.

On one occasion we were told that a missing inmate could hardly walk 100 yards and was not in possession of any money. Three dog handlers searched the hospital grounds for two days to no avail, only to be informed at the end of the second day that the missing inmate had been found in Piccadilly in the west end of London. He explained to the police officer who found him wandering about the streets, that he was looking for a woman (weren't we all). Claybury to Piccadilly is well over 6 miles and for a man over 70 years, supposedly only being able to walk 100 yards, this was pretty good going.

Another search for a missing inmate occurred on a typically, blustery, miserable March day and not the best time of the year to be out all night. We started our search at about 2pm with three handlers, only stopping when the dogs were tired and when night was closing in.

The search started again at 8am the next morning, once again with three dogs and handlers. It was not too long before my dog 'Zola' indicated a thick clump of holly and began to bark. It took me sometime to claw my way through to the centre of the bushes to be greeted by the sight of a man lying in the thicket with a jacket over his face. I presumed (wrongly) that this was our missing inmate, who because of his advanced age and thin clothing, had died as a result of hyperthermia and it was too late to attempt resuscitation. I took out my printed description form, to check his details and pulled the jacket from his face only to be greeted by my corpse saying "How did the Arsenal get on?"

We did many more searches of these grounds before it became a very upmarket housing development.

The show must go on and did
By RAY PECKHAM

I was fortunate indeed when, as an Inspector in charge of police dogs in the north and east area of London, I was deputed to supervise the display of dog handling at the Royal Tournament. The Metropolitan Police did not have a demonstration team as such and dogs were selected from those that could be spared from street duty for a short time. Consequently things could sometimes get 'interesting' during our performances.

Let me set the scene, which on this occasion is behind the scenes. Those of you with memories of the Royal Tournament will remember that at one end of the arena was a mock-up of a huge castle entrance through which the performers would enter and perform their acts, always with admirable military precision. In order that the show flows evenly, without any breaks in the programme of events, the succession of performers are lined up in the sequence of their entrance behind a huge black curtain, which prevents the public from seeing them before they are ready to march into the arena.

So picture the scene behind the curtain when the Metropolitan Police 'Demonstration Team' (as we called it) fell into line, ready to march off. The handlers all in their best 'bibs and tuckers', and the dogs well wound-up with all the excitement in the air. Behind the dog team was the All American University marching band, male and female, all immaculately turned out with rifles at the slope and musical instruments at the ready. Now behind those were the horses (also well wound-up) of the Royal Horse Artillery, with their limbers and field guns. Now the tricky part is to get them all on, in their turn, without the following act being seen by the public, so the dog team squashed up close together so that the aforesaid curtain could be pulled across behind them.

Our cue came to go on. The lights went out and the arena and the holding area was plunged into sudden darkness. With the roar of the crowd and the dogs now excited almost to fever pitch, off leash, and about to march in a tight group into the darkness, handlers couldn't see a hand in front of them. This was the cue for a massive punch-up. The noise was deafening. The horses started to rear and kick. The All American University band scattered in all directions, instruments and rifles flying. Several dogs bolted into the arena and refused all commands from their handlers to recall. The really nasty dog that was being kept back for the armed bandit chase finale decided to join in the fun and bit his handler on the arm and his hand. Blood was spurting everywhere. The handler, somewhat surprised at being bitten by his own dog, dropped the lead leaving the dog to look around for another target. Luckily I was able to grab the lead and pull the dog away to one side.

The handlers as usual rose to the occasion and marched on into the arena as if nothing had happened. Some gathered their dogs as they went while two handlers collected the wrong dog but still pressed on with the show. I needed to get into the arena ready to take the salute when the dogs lined up at the end of the performance so I had to get rid of the attack dog that had caused the injury. I saw a Chief Superintendent standing in the holding area so I said "Hang on to this until I get back" The handler was on his way to St Thomas's Hospital by ambulance. The dogs performed well and we all marched off to thunderous applause after Tom Tanner did a fantastic double barrel armed attack with a dog on each arm. The band had reformed, the Royal Horse Artillery horses had calmed down although there was a lot of nervousness about when we withdrew behind the big black curtain.

No, the tragic evening doesn't end there. Where was the Chief Superintendent with the blood thirsty attack-dog? I then discovered that he had decided to 'pop out' into the public area to let the people see the nice dog he had acquired. He was in a circle of children with a queue waiting to stroke the lovely police doggy.

There's more.

It was customary for the officer in charge of a display team to proceed to a lift cage to be taken up to the Royal Box. I duly did this and an army sergeant major let me into the lift, turned out the light and together we ascended to the Royal Box which was in darkness as a security precaution. When the lift stopped he said nothing so I stepped out into the darkness, tripped over the step and straight into a lady's lap. A female voice I recognised said "Oh those dogs" I will take to my grave the remainder of the story........

'Silas' the circus dog
By JOE LANCASTER

One evening during the late 1950s, during a late turn duty at Plaistow police station, I was called to a block of offices in Plashet Grove, West Ham, where local officers believed that a breaking had occurred at a block of offices and that the suspect may still be on the premises. It was about 9.15pm and it was quite dark. I took my dog 'Silas' into the yard at the rear of the building and there I saw a ladder leaning against a wall.

I decided to check that first so I put 'Silas' into the "down" and started to climb the ladder. When I was about six rungs from the top I heard a panting sound behind me. Looking down I saw that 'Silas' was climbing the ladder behind me. The hairs on the back of my neck stood up and I froze. There was 'Silas', as happy as could be and so pleased to be with his mate. Thoughts raced through my mind. What if he falls or jumps off, what if he killed himself or got badly injured. How would I ever stop filling reports. Worst of all how would I explain to my wife and children what I had done to 'their' dog. This was every dog handler's nightmare.

I thought to myself "in for a penny, in for a pound" and could think of no alternative but to continue my climb and hope for the best, I didn't dare say a word. When I reached the roof 'Silas' was right behind me and climbed onto the roof behind me. The edge was about 14 inches wide and covered with asphalt. I grabbed him with a vice like grip on his collar.

Now my dilemma was how on earth was I going to get him down. The only option was to carry him down so I picked him up. This sounds easier than it was. Full grown German shepherd dogs do not take kindly to being picked up, and being thrown onto my back and being held tightly by his legs was not a happy experience for him. Taking a deep breath I started to descend the ladder while 'Silas' struggled to get off. It was the longest descent of a ladder in my life. When we were a few rungs from the bottom 'Silas' won his battle and jumped the last few feet, fortunately without injury. I then took my second breath.

I would like to inform all interested persons that this was the best kept secret of my police service, and was witnessed only by two local 'bobbies' who seem to think that what they had seen was something that our dogs were trained to do. Fortunately this experience didn't get to the ears of my senior officers, or of Keston, the dog section headquarters, so no reports were necessary.

Encores were definitely out of the question and my mate 'Silas' lived to a ripe old age.

Calling all cars

By JEFF TERRY

The subject of this true story shall remain nameless (he can own up later if he so wishes) suffice to say that he smokes a pipe and has the drollest of humours.

Mid-week early turn and the Area Dog Inspector was visiting the Area Dog Unit at Forest Gate to conduct an Annual Appraisal with one of the dog handlers. He also had another Appraisal to conduct, this being the other officer who was posted to Juliet Zero dog van, which at that time was patrolling the area of Chingford for burglars. The Inspector, considering it more expedient for him to remain where he was, had made a call requesting that the dog van attend Forest Gate for the meeting. The dog van attended as directed and the crew member referred to above was led through an hour long appraisal.

Now, whether it was the mere fact of being on early turn or whether it was the assumption in his mind that the appraisal could have waited for a more suitable time (which wouldn't have inconvenienced either party), wasn't clear. But, whatever the reason, it caused the recently appraised officer to drive back to his allotted ground whilst bending the ear of his colleague. The diatribe entered into castigated the idiocy of 'Having to drive all the way to Forest Gate,' 'Couldn't it have waited till he came to J,' 'What an absolute waste of petrol' and 'After twenty odd years in the force why do they have to keep giving me a stupid appraisal'. So on and so on, with the occasional word which has been banned by the BBC until after the watershed.

After a quite a lengthy period of time another voice entered the cab of the dog van. This one belonged to the controller at Information Room at New Scotland Yard. It was a polite message which was intended to be helpful. "Would the R/T unit with the depressed clip on their radio handset and who are discussing how well their Appraisal went care to rectify the position!"

The new recruit

By ROD CROWHURST

Back in 1969, I was the proud beneficiary of a police dog puppy, which had been bred at the Dog Training Establishment from working parents. At this time, the puppy programme was being overseen by Sergeant Bob Plumridge, a man with a vast knowledge of working dogs in general and police dogs in particular.

Each month I attended the DTE with my puppy and each month Bob assessed our progress to date and instructed us on what we should be doing to further the dog's development during the coming month. He was very keen that our pups were exposed to everything that they could be expected to come into contact with during their working lives, thus I spent many hours gently coaxing the dog into tackling things like open stairways, fire escapes, shiny floors, etc. In addition to this, I also undertook trips on buses and trains, took the dog into busy market places and children's playgrounds – I even participated in a TV programme about working dogs. In short, I covered all of the angles and duly graduated from DTE at the top of my class.

Two days later I reported for duty at Forest Gate Police Station for a late turn and I can still remember the pride I felt when I stepped out of the station yard (we patrolled on foot in those days) and turned into Green Street on patrol – the yobbery of East London didn't know what was about to hit them!

The first 200 yards passed without incident, the dog walking along at heel on a nicely looped lead and I was king of all I surveyed until I became aware of the fact that I was suddenly yanked backwards as the dog came to a shuddering halt. I looked at him and he was quite a sight with his hackles raised and his tail firmly between his legs – talk about 'fight or flight' – the one thing that was certain was that he wasn't going to take another step in the direction I wanted to travel.

It took a little while for me to establish the cause of his discomfort – after all, we were only passing a garden supplies shop.

This particular shop, in addition to selling seeds, plants and fertilisers, also sold garden gnomes and there, not six feet away, was the cause of the dog's discomfort – a family of garden gnomes with eye levels on a par with the dogs. I quickly discovered that the sight of a fully booted and suited policeman, obviously having a problem with his rough tough police dog, naturally draws a crowd – when the crowd ascertained the source of the problem, it seemed to amuse them and I returned to the safety of the police station, not quite as proudly as I had left it. As for the dog, I think 'shamefaced' would best describe his expression. He did become a 'cracker' though and the yobs weren't laughing for long.

Who told you to get that dog mate?

By DENNIS WALLAND

My first day at the Dog School, together with Rusty Nightingale and Tony Andrews, I found myself standing by the kennels, full of apprehension mixed with the unbounded joy that at last I was on the first rung to being a dog handler. This was called a "suitability course" and was to last a week.

Our first task was to take the "annual leave" dogs for an "emptying" walk and as I entered the kennel area, a sudden wave of fear came over me. I had been taught some valuable lessons regarding the sharp ends of police dogs, and to see what looked to me like a pack of raging lions, throwing themselves at the wire fronts of their compounds was the most terrifying sight I had ever seen,

I needed to be a bit clever here so I hatched a cunning plan. I would look for the quietest dog and I would start with him. I picked 'Digger'. He was probably the oldest dog in the job and it seemed that he could just about stand up. I put him on the lead and we set off up the 'patch'. He was fine and seemed happy to be out of his cage.

Then disaster struck.

The kennel-man said "Who told you to take that dog out mate?" I said "No one told me to, I just took him, why?" We don't take him out mate," he said, "Why not? He seemed alright when I got him out", "Yes he is alright when you get him out, it's when you try to put him back he'll 'do' you."

Oh s**t, what have I done? I walked 'Digger' to the front gate, then back towards the kennels, then back to the front gate, then back towards the kennels. Digger was beginning to get slower and I thought if I can tire him out, he won't want to "do" me quite so painfully.

The others had shouted that it was tea time and I waved to acknowledge I had heard them and I would be along in a minute. Another walk down to the front gate might be enough to guarantee my safe withdrawal from this desperate situation. It was on the way back that I looked up towards the canteen window and there saw some very amused faces all having a good laugh at my expense. I put 'Digger' back in his kennel and he was absolutely delighted to be out of the hands of this idiot novice and just flopped down knackered and breathing a sigh of relief.

Twenty years later, I was saying to novices "Who told you to take that dog out mate, just wait till you try and put him back!"

His name was Ernie, and he 'worked' the wildest police dog in the east
by DENNIS WALLAND

Ernie Baxter was a legend.

Ernie's first dog, Amber belonged to the early days of the section when all a police dog needed to do was bite people, and that included villains, policemen and any casual bystander who happened to be within range. A dog for the time of teddy boys, razor gangs, cosh boys and the wild bunch which World War II had not tamed. Consequently 'Amber' was feared by all.

When 'Amber' finally passed on, Ernie vowed that his next dog would be nothing like his first and began a routine of giving the dog more freedom, working on the theory that his temperament would not suffer from too much pressure by his handler.

It was under this relaxed regime that 'Tiger', or as Ernie called him Tiiigeeer, came to be. Here was a dog to which the restraints of police discipline, or even normal dog owning formalities, were strangers.

An example of this would be when working on the dog van with Ernie, we would go into Barking, Ernie's police station, for refreshments. As we got out of the van, Ernie would open the back cage of the van and out would jump Tiger. We walked up the stairs to the canteen, while Tiger took himself off on a stroll round the town. He would eventually return and after just popping down into the cellars to have a pee on Keith Murray's locker, (he was the other dog handler at Barking, and his locker was easily recognised by the smell, and the fact that the bottom three feet was rusty) Tiger would then make his way up to the canteen and woe betide anybody who left his meal anywhere within reach.

Such was the happy relationship between man and dog which either amused you, or embarrassed you, according to where you were and who the other witnesses were.

After waiting for the key-holder to arrive at Bodgers Store in Ilford, where the alarm bell was ringing, we entered to search, accompanied by the key-holder and most of the relief at Ilford police station. Tiger immediately went over to a roll of expensive carpet and cocked his leg on this imaginary tree. "That's nice" said the disgruntled key-holder. "I suppose you'll be banging that out cheap now" said Ernie "I might be interested in it, my dog obviously likes it" The relief shuffled giggling from the building, and I asked the key-holder to wait outside, fearful of what Tiger would do next, and knowing there was worse to come, and there was, but that is known as my "number twos" story and in deference to Ernie must remain our secret.

One sunny summer afternoon, Ernie was walking in the back streets of Barking through a housing estate. Tiger of course was off the lead, walking on the other side of the street and carrying out olfactory inspections of all the lamp-posts and gate posts. Concentrating on his work Tiger was suddenly surprised by a citizen who walked down his front path and opened his gate in a perfectly lawful manner, just as Tiger was concentrating on some delicious smell on the gate post. Being startled, Tiger then reacted in the time honoured fashion by biting said citizen on the upper leg. The shout brought the matter to the attention of Ernie who had been similarly deep in thought on his own side of the street. Being in policeman's uniform Ernie thought he had better go over and see what was occurring. "What happened?" Ernie asked "I've just been bitten by that dog" came the reply. "It is obviously a stray", said Ernie, "luckily I have this dog lead in my pocket, I'll take it down the police station, goodbye" When the victim went to the police station to see if anybody had claimed the dog, and who was the owner to be sued, strangely the Station Officer could find no trace of the dog or Ernie.

Send in the dogs
By PETER FORSTER

I have worked and trained dogs for over forty years, both in the Police and civilian working trials. In 1990, I was a member of the Metropolitan Police Dog Demonstration Team. The team were asked to perform at the Royal Tournament at Earls Court in their Centenary year. It was a great honour for a civilian Police Service to be asked to perform at the Royal Tournament.

Major Mike Parker, the producer of the 100th Royal Tournament, asked us for a show that was away from the usual dog display performances. We started to get ideas together and work towards having a performance that was to have dogs running from different directions and passing through and over a car at the same time, dogs running into old type police boxes and retrieving the phone, car chases with police dogs attacking all sorts of armed criminals etc. The main part of the show was a building that sheltered armed terrorists who had taken a hostage, with an assault on the building by handlers who abseiled from the roof with the dogs attached by a special harness to the handler's waist. The performance was spectacular and very slick which played to a packed audience at every show.

There had to be in-fills whilst equipment was lowered into the arena and this is where I and my dog 'Casca', together with another handler and dog came in. 'Casca' had only just finished a basic dog training course and was not a seasoned dog for attack work. We decided that the two dogs, one at each end of the arena, would be sent forward to retrieve a rubber ring that had been thrown into the air from a sprung device when the dog jumped on a step at the front. The dog would catch the ring and return to the handler with it. A simple exercise, but the training of the dog took many hours to ensure it performed the exercise fast and without any problems or delays. The higher the ring went, the louder the audience clapped and cheered. We would then leave the arena quickly as the next part of the performance was already beginning.

This exercise went well for the ten days of the Tournament with the cheers and applause of the audience getting louder each time the dogs caught the ring. If you have attended the Royal Tournament you may know that at the last performance, despite warnings from Major Mike Parker and his team for no fooling around, things go 'deliberately' wrong. For example, the Royal Marines would fire their guns into the air whilst going through their marching routine and rubber hens and bird feathers would fall from the roof. The bandsmen would strike their large kettle drums, only to have clouds of dust go into the air at each beat of the drum. The gun crews would be wearing bow ties whilst racing from one end of the arena to the other. All this from other performers was going on, but what could happen to a dog catching a rubber ring from the sprung device? Nothing at all, I convinced myself.

Well, our part of the performance came and apart from noticing that more than the usual number of military personnel had gathered to watch the two dogs perform, I thought no more of it. When both handlers and dogs were in place at each end of the arena, we sent our dogs forward to hit the pedal, see the ring fly out, be caught by the dogs in mid air and return to the handler with rapturous applause from the audience. However, it never quite went like that, 'Casca' caught the ring in mid air, but immediately dropped it to the ground and begun to tear at the ring with his teeth. I called for the dog to return to me, but he continued to search the ground for something that he was very keen to get again. Unknown to me the troops had taped a large piece of steak to the inside of the ring and 'Casca' was really enjoying it. I called 'Casca' again; as I could see that the handler at the other end of the arena had finished and was waiting to leave the arena. I have always said during my years of dog training "A dog will learn something every day, better by training than by accident." Learning by accident had now taken on a new meaning for 'Casca' who had now returned to the device and was hitting the pedal, constantly with both paws and looking in the air for the next piece of steak to appear. He refused to stop hitting the pedal and I had to go to 'Casca' and pull him away with the audience in constant laughter at the antics of the dog.

When out of the arena I asked the other handler if his dog had steak taped to the inside of the rubber ring. He said that he had no problems and the dog had just retrieved the ring. I thought that was the end of the prank as we had a good laugh about it. At the end of the performance, four teams of four handlers and dogs entered the arena from each corner. The handlers would march in; marching is always difficult for Police Officers, with their dogs off-lead walking to heel. Everything was back on track with no more stunts; well, that was only after the handlers that came from the roof to attack the terrorists had appeared dressed as Superman, Batman and Robin. What Major Parker was doing at that time, one could only guess and I am sure that we would have been invited back one day, if only the Blair Government had not stopped such a spectacular annual event.

Anyway, back to the march in! Casca and I were now at the other end of the arena to where our steak performance had taken place. We were about half way into the arena when Casca actually broke from the ranks because his highly trained nose had located the other piece of steak on the ground. This was the piece of steak that the other handler's dog had missed because it had parted from the rubber ring when it was thrown into the air. 'Casca' decided that this was too good to miss and only joined me in time for the final finally. Well, the audience enjoyed it and we finished to a standing ovation.

Another day ends in the life of a handler and his dog or should that be a dog and his handler!

The joys of training
By JOHN BARRETT

My first basic course at Keston was with a bitch called "Zola", a great working partner, who was both a family friend and a hard working Police Dog. During this course we had to do a week's late turn in order to give the dog experience of working in the dark.

One night about 8pm it was decided by the Instructor that we would try a night chase on the field at the Dog School. We all went with our dogs to the field and our Instructor told me to pad up so that I could do the first run. My right arm was padded with some old fire hose and then some bits of rag from an old jacket. Being a field we had no street lights, so it was dark and I mean dark. I started to walk and the handler called me to stop. I replied with a few chosen words suggesting I was not all that keen on hanging around and started to run down the field.

The handler called out that if I did not stop he would send his dog, but I kept running. He then shouted to his dog "Stop him." So far so good! I held my right arm out in order to give the dog more of a chance on his first night time chase. As he got nearer I could hear movement among the grass and knew he was close. All at once he got me, but not my right arm as he had been taught. He was hanging onto my behind with a full set of teeth. I bellowed out a few chosen words and cursed the Instructor, the handler, the dog and a number of other persons who were not present, but the pain remained. The dog must have recognised the instruction to let go because he did and I was left holding both hands on my behind to ease the pain. I was not asked to run any more that night, I doubt if I would have done had I been asked.

Now that's what I call "a real pain in the a**e."

I was on my third basic course with a Dog called "Bodie" (the name taken from the TV programme Bodie and Doyle). We were doing a continuation track across the fields of Kent, one dog actually tracking, the other four from the class following behind. When the tracking dog indicated he had found an article we changed places, the tracking dog going to the rear and the next dog picking up the track.

I was last in the line and we went up a small incline to a group of trees with a small fence around them. The track continued into the trees as did the lead dog, the others following. When I came to the fence I saw a small gap to the left and went through it. I had only taken about four steps when I found myself going down into slurry. As I was sinking I seem to remember the dog using me as some sort of ladder to save himself (Intelligent animal!). When the slurry reached my shoulders; the dog just stood and looked at me as if I had gone mad.

I then started to curse the instructor, the dog, the Dog School and all and sundry. Then the other dog handlers came back and I had to wait until they had stopped laughing before I was dragged out. It was decided that I had better go back to the van that had got us to the starting point of the track. The driver agreed to take me back to the Dog School but only if I didn't sit down in the van and mess the seats up.

On my arrival back at Keston they put the hose on me and then I was given some overalls. I then drove home. My wife was not impressed with the smell and offered to make a bed up in the kennel. She also refused to put my dirty clothes in **our** washing machine.

This East London boy learnt some important lessons about the countryside.

Bent baker from the Bakers Arms

By HARRY FELL

I was on duty with John Barrett patrolling in Juliet Zero dog van. We knew that some nefarious act was being committed on a regular basis by a baker at a shop near the Bakers Arms at Leyton. This was occurring early in the morning so we took up a position in a side street from where we could keep observation.

After a considerable wait, we saw a lorry draw up outside the shop and saw the driver unload several bags of flour before driving off.

I went into the shop whilst John followed and stopped the lorry.

In the shop I found the flour and eventually when the baker was questioned he was unable to produce any invoices for the flour delivery, as was the lorry driver unable to satisfy John as to the legitimacy of the transaction. Both men were arrested, one for theft and the other for receiving stolen property.

Some time later the case came before Snaresbrook Crown Court where both men pleaded "Not guilty".

Just before the case started I discovered to my horror that I did not have my pocket book with my notes which I had taken at the time of the crime. This was serious because I may not have been able to remember all the important details of day, date, time etc and the case might be lost. John and I had made our notes together in the canteen at the time of the arrest. Together we hatched a cunning plan that when John, who would give evidence first, left the witness box he would leave his pocket book on the stand so that I could use it to refresh my memory with the relevant details. This was quite legal, but could cause embarrassment if brought to notice and would certainly cause some form of rebuke from the judge.

I started to give my evidence when I noticed a slight disturbance happening in the jury box. I glanced at John and he was sitting up straight, going a funny shade of pale. A note was being passed from a juror along the row towards the usher and thence to the judge. Beads of sweat were forming and a nasty feeling began to grow in my stomach because by now I had also seen what was happening and was certain the subterfuge had been discovered.

The Judge stopped me in the middle of my evidence and my heart thumped like a drum. John started to slump down in his seat in the hope that he would disappear in some kind of vapour.

"Would juror number seven stand up please" said the judge. Up stood juror number seven. "Do you know this man" said the judge to me. I gulped audibly and replied "Yes my lord, he lives in a house next door to my allotment," the Judge asked "Is he a friend of yours officer?" "Not as such" I replied, the colour returning to my cheeks "we have chatted over the fence about gardening but that is all" "In that case" said the judge "we will continue with the trial" After this frightener I decided not to look at John's pocket book any more and was so delighted when I had finished and left the box on my wobbly legs, promising myself that I would never forget my pocket book again.

Both men were found guilty and dealt with and the case became known as the 'Bent Baker of the Bakers Arms'

"Smart Sergeant. Smart Dogs. Shame about the handlers."
Basic dog course at Keston 1957/58

'Henry' – the worst police dog ever

By DENNIS WALLAND

He was my dog, so I can say that whilst I would have defended him to the death at the time.

His story began when I was a Continuation Training Instructor at Avery Hill, south east area. My working dog, 'Nimbus' was retired, so although my days were taken up with helping others train their dogs, I was getting bored. One of the dogs in the classes, a Weimaraner, was really clever and I was so impressed that I splashed out the money and bought 'Henry', a Weimaraner, for myself, with the intention of training him for civilian working trials which I did with a reasonable result. He would do all that I asked of him and we were both happy.

Then I ruined it all when, after arresting a couple of car thieves whilst off duty, I realised how much I missed the razzmatazz of the job and I applied to go back to street duty. Since I had a ready-made dog, which the job accepted free of cost, my wish was granted. My mistake was that I forgot to consult 'Henry.' This was not, in his opinion, a suitable occupation and was certainly a humiliation for a dog of such distinguished breeding.

On the basic course he messed up everything he did. All those exercises that were a piece of cake as a civilian dog were treated with distain and a complete lack of interest. We just managed to pass out and I was off to J Division with all the optimism that, once we were out of the dog school, things would get better.

So:

The Property Seek

First day on early turn I took 'Henry' to Epping Forest for a good long walk. Setting off I searched my pockets for an article that I could throw out and search for when we came back after the walk. Nothing could be found except the keys to the dog van. Alarm bells rang but not loud enough. So, aware of the danger of the dog not being able to find such an important article, I carefully dropped them in the undergrowth making sure that I would be able to find them if the dog failed. Wasn't I clever to take that precaution?

Back after the walk, I set 'Henry' to search with the minimum of trepidation. Success, he found the keys almost instantly and came back and sat in front of me holding them in his mouth. "Good Boy", I said, which must have been the incentive for him to give me a strange look as the keys disappeared from sight down his throat. "Oh S**t!"

Then followed a most embarrassing 'car to car' radio conversation with dog sergeant Moren. I wanted him to come and meet me and he definitely wanted me to meet him! Eventually I had the humiliating experience of having to admit to the entire Metropolitan Police District on the radio "my bloody dog has swallowed the van keys". I will leave the comments of others to your imagination.

It cost me quite a lot of money for replacement keys and three days of concern whilst waiting for nature to take its course. Just before I took 'Henry' to the vets and further humiliation, I found the keys in the garden. Not in the brown stuff as I had expected but very neatly wrapped up in blades of grass and camouflaged. So even at this stage 'Henry' was trying to have me over. I hated him!

The Chase
The one thing that 'Henry' was prepared to do for me was the 'chase'. At training and in demonstrations he did well, so I was confident that he wouldn't let me down out on the streets.

Our first night duty, which incidentally he disliked with a vengeance refusing to come out of his kennel if it was dark, I found myself in the dog van on my own. 'Henry' was in the front cage with the door open ready to burst into action at the slightest opportunity.

I saw a car and didn't like the look of the driver so on went the blue light. He was off at speed with me following at the best speed a dog van could do (which was not a lot). Working a different area to the one I was used to I had no idea where I was but followed gamely. By good fortune, the runaway drove into a cul-de-sac and then jumped out and ran away.

Oh joy; this was what dog handling was all about. I screeched to a halt and leapt out, calling 'Henry' as I did so. I saw him out of the corner of my eye jumping over the seat but I didn't see him again. "Stop him!" I shouted several times until I realised I was on my own and started to feel a bit silly.

Those were the days when I was still capable of the occasional run and I caught the villain and after a struggle brought him back to the van.

There to my delight, was 'Henry', curled up on my nice warm comfortable seat. He had the effrontery to open just one eye and look at me with his "You stupid idiot" look. I hated him even more.

The only good thing was that the runaway driver admitted he had no tax or insurance so I gave him a verbal warning and let him go. There was no way I was going to go to court and tell that story.

The Seek

Saturday morning about 8.30 and I received a call to some playing fields somewhere in the depths of darkest Walthamstow to search for a hand-bag snatcher. The precise location being a football field on a plateau with a steep drop down at the edge. A wire netting fence at the bottom made it an enclosed area. The 'baddie' could have been down there and so it seemed to me a good idea to send my police dog to search this area, after all, isn't that what they are supposed to do?

"Find him" I said. 'Henry' looked at the drop, saw it was thick undergrowth with nasty brambles and nettles. He looked at me and his look said "Get stuffed, I'm not going down there". "Oh yes you are" said I and to encourage him, I grabbed his collar in one hand and his rear quarters in the other hand and propelled him into this jungle. He stopped, stiff legged and looked at me with his "You b*****d look". He then very gingerly made his way to the bottom.

After lots of encouragement from me he then gave such a wonderfully deep bark. It was the kind of bark that gives all dog handlers such a thrill because it means there is somebody there and job done. In my excitement I jumped down the slope, completely oblivious to the cuts and scratches I was getting from the brambles and made my way to where the barking had been coming from.

Only then did I realise that 'Henry' had stopped barking. Then to my delight, I found him standing at the top of the hill looking down at me saying "Gotcha!". Of course, there was nobody there. I climbed back up the slope and perhaps the look on my face told 'Henry' it would be a good idea to hare it back to the dog van. Now I really do hate him.

Sometimes people ask me why I retired after 25 years and didn't stay on to do 30 years. Now you know!

"Two 16 stone men plus two 90lb dogs.
Never mind how we got out – how did we get in?"
BMC mini van used as a dog van from early 1969

The legend that was Frank Dew

By DENNIS WALLAND

Frank Dew was certainly entitled to take his place among the legends of the dog section. He was an individual who was admired by most, and feared by others, (some of whom were his colleagues, but didn't really know him well). He was forthright in speech, not suffering fools gladly and given to vivid and colourful descriptions of anyone who crossed him in any way. He was a 'hard' man which I came to better understand when at his funeral the story was told of his childhood, he having been brought up in an orphanage under conditions that would certainly not be allowed these days. He had served in the army as a drill instructor at Colchester Military Prison, and I can best describe him as a cross between Mr Mckay from "Porridge", and Captain Mainwaring from "Dad's Army" when addressing Private Pike "You stupid boy" The difference with Frank was that Pike would have been a self abuser.

His courage could not be questioned, a fact that was borne out when during a period of ten days, a group of 'travellers/gipsies' celebrated the death of one of their number by going on a drunken rampage, smashing up every pub in the area and finally came to rest at the "Compasses" pub at Hornchurch which just happened to be Frank's local. The landlord called upon Frank (knowing he was a policeman) for help and Frank, after sending for assistance from Hornchurch police station, stepped alone into the bar, well knowing that he was going to get hurt, which he did, suffering a fractured skull for his trouble. As he said afterwards "I couldn't just stand there and watch them smash the place up, the reputation of the job was at stake".

He was always smart and meticulous in his appearance when on or off duty, which makes my story about him even more pertinent than the same story would be if it were about anybody else.

Frank was a keen darts player and played regularly for the team at the "Compasses" public house.

Frank's dog at this time was called 'Condor' and like Frank he was an individual kind of animal. He hated any other beast that possessed four legs whether it was cat, dog or camel, with a passion which caused Frank all kinds of problems. Frank was equal to the challenge but it involved taking special precautions when exercising 'Condor'

It was Frank's habit to take 'Condor' for a last walk before retiring for the night. Bearing in mind 'Condor's' attitude to other animals, to avoid any problems Frank had made an arrangement with a local school caretaker that in return for exclusive use of the school playing fields Frank would patrol around the premises, thus ensuring that no villains were about. An arrangement which was of great benefit to both parties.

It was on such a night that after enjoying a late game of darts Frank let himself into the playing fields and sent 'Condor' off into the night for a last run. Deep in thought Frank wandered about nonchalantly.

"Strange", thought Frank, "I am sure I can hear thunder. They didn't forecast that for tonight." The thunder got nearer and nearer when suddenly from out of the darkness came a dozen galloping gipsy horses being hotly pursued by 'Condor'. Frank jumped out of the way and shouted to 'Condor' who was oblivious to the command and continued out of sight and hearing, still in hot pursuit.

After a couple of minutes the sound of thunder returned and again from the gloom came this stampede complete with 'Condor' (now really enjoying himself) passing by Frank, who was now beginning to get a bit excited himself.

No response to Frank's shouted commands, and off again into the darkness went this galloping horde.

The same thing happened again with the thundering steeds galloping round the entire school building, but on the third circuit something was missing. No 'Condor'

Frank was now beginning to lose the feeling of happy contentment he had felt earlier and a small rage was bubbling up in his chest.

"Where the bleep has that bleeping dog got to?"

He waited, working out how he was planning to repay this bleeping animal for his misbehaviour, but the dog didn't come. A small shiver of fear entered Frank's hard heart as he wondered just what the dog was up to now.

He called – no response. Panic now set in and Frank went off into the darkness to search for his dog. Picking his way through an area where contractors had been digging holes whilst laying a new gas main in the ground, Frank had the bright idea of getting his dog to bark. "Speak" he ordered and then he heard a muffled bark. Again and again Frank commanded, the dog responded, Frank getting nearer until he discovered 'Condor' had fallen down a hole in the ground and was now about eight feet down a mud-filled shaft. Frank could just make out the dog by the dim lights of the nearby street lamps.

What Frank called his dog now you will never know because it is not suitable to be repeated, but Frank quickly realised that he needed help in this matter.

It was not within Frank's remit to get help from somebody who might tell the story to others and thereby cause him embarrassment, but there was one person he knew that he could rely on to keep this secret.

Unfortunately, June his loving wife, was in bed. Undeterred he left 'Condor' to his self inflicted misery and walked the short distance home telling June to put on a coat over her night attire and to follow him. History does not record what she said.

Frank's plan was to take a torch, his tracking harness and line and, using a ladder he had noticed laying nearby, he would go down the ladder, put the harness on the dog and with the line attached climb back up the ladder and pull the dog out of the hole. Cleverly Frank remembered the mud at the bottom of the hole and he had put his Wellington boots on so that he would not get his clothes muddy. June's role was to stand at the top of the hole and shine the torch down so Frank could see what he was doing. June also needed to hold the end of the tracking line, waiting for Frank's reappearance from the hole, after which they could all go home.

All went well, until after climbing down the ladder, Frank was about to put the harness on 'Condor', when June dropped the torch into the mud. It went out and was never seen again. In the melee 'Condor' started to struggle violently, covering Frank with the mucky grey slime. Frank's mood by now had changed and I think he was getting angry. It didn't make him any happier when, as he started to climb the ladder, off came his Wellington boots, but he continued his climb in his socks to feel the ladder was slowly sinking into the mud and now the top of the ladder was sufficiently below the top of the pit as to make escape impossible.

This evening was not exactly going to plan and the blame was being laid at the feet of 'Condor' and June equally, since there was nobody else there.

Now Frank had to think of a way out of this and the only solution was for June to pull the dog up then go for help from another source, but not to let too many people know about this debacle or Frank's credibility as a hard man could be damaged beyond repair.

He instructed June on the action she was to take. She was to take 'Condor' home, then phone Hornchurch police station and ask to speak to the van driver, and tell him, and him alone, to come and help. He was to bring a ladder. Frank knew that he would be able to instruct the van driver that this incident was to remain a secret and, depending how much the van driver feared upsetting Frank, there was still a chance that this story would not be told elsewhere.

June did as she was told, well almost, because not unreasonably, given the circumstances, she said "Frank needs assistance". Now this is "police-speak" for "officer in trouble, everybody come and help him". The next thing Frank heard from his watery grave was the sound of the bell on the van as it left the station picking up PCs on the way.

When it arrived, the entire relief was there, ready to go into action to save Frank from whatever dangerous situation he had got himself into. Looking down the hole, and seeing our hero entirely covered in mud with steam coming out of his nose, mouth and ears must have caused the kind of mirth that grown men find hard to control, especially policemen. Frank couldn't speak for rage; the others couldn't speak for laughing.

The wonderful thing about Frank was that, although the other PCs found the whole business incredibly amusing, in no way did it diminish the respect in which they all held him, and it was never mentioned again – at least not in Frank's presence.

Window shopping

By NORMAN MASON

I was on duty with my with Police dog 'Denver' in Palmers Green N13 when at about 2am we were called to a shopbreaking in Green Lanes.

One side of the road had shops; on the other side were large Victorian houses, each with a front garden about 10 yards long and leading up to a large ground floor window. While we were searching two men ran out of the shop premises. Officers from the area car were able to catch one, the other ran across the road and went straight though a ground floor window, followed by 'Denver'. I was following.

Unbeknown to me there was a couple in bed immediately under the window and when I went through the man shouted out "How many more", I said "Sorry mate" and called off my dog who was hanging onto the prisoner by the seat of his trousers. The couple in the bed were covered in glass but had no injuries apart from being very embarrassed.

I saw the young lady some days later while I was out shopping and I asked if she was OK. She went a beautiful shade of red and assured me she was OK and so was her partner.

When the evidence was given at the committal I saw a few grins from the Magistrates.

Things that go bump in the night

By RAY PECKHAM

Night duty and I was on duty in the dog van with Jack Mulford. About two or three in the morning we decided to give our dogs a run so we went up to High Beach in Epping Forest.

When we arrived we stopped on the grassed area overlooking the valley, where there was a steep incline into the forest. Lo and behold there was a Dormobile van parked facing the valley and in total darkness. I got out of our van and walked to the vehicle nearside door...looked in....pitch dark. I pulled back the sliding door wide enough to put my head in. The stench was appalling.

Then I made out the lower parts of a female, then another on the other side. On the lower part of the vehicle were two further females all in states of undress in very compromising positions. A female screamed – someone tried to get up and knocked off the handbrake – vehicle started rolling towards the valley – I grabbed the leading edge of the door. The door shot towards the back of the vehicle. Now, unbeknown to me Jack had arrived on scene and, seeing what was about to happen, had grabbed the vehicle just towards the rear of the door. Door now slid back and Jack screamed out. I let go of my door to see what had happened to Jack. Jack had his hand trapped in the door and was moving with the van towards the valley at a fair old rate of knots. His dog was barking-girls were screaming – Jack was shouting – vehicle passed over my foot just as someone applied the handbrake.

End result:
ADVICE GIVEN

Entry in stop book:
Bleeding hand – bruised foot.

Who's looking for whom?

By JOHN BARRETT

On duty, late turn, on Juliet Zero (the Dog Van), I was working with Dennis Walland and his new dog 'Henry', a very young Weimaraner. The dog was very sleek and you could imagine him looking into shop windows to see his own reflection as he passed. This was one of the dog's first tours of duty

It was very quiet on the radio and not a lot for us to deal with, so we decided to give the dogs some training and drove to the Water Works in Leyton. The gates are always open but very rarely are there any workers about and this was an excellent place to train our dogs in 'the search for a person' exercise.

We parked the van and I wandered off to hide for 'Henry'. I found a low brick wall and lay down behind it. This was a very easy seek for the dog but I had taken into account that he was still very young.

I heard Dennis give the command, "Find him" and I waited quietly in my hiding place. After a short period of time, I heard 'Henry' come padding around the corner and I then heard him stop on the other side of the wall. The wall was very low and he could have looked over if he wanted to but, he just stood very still. He had clearly got the first part of the exercise right and detected me using his sense of smell, but had forgotten the second part; he now needed to pass the information onto Dennis, namely by barking. But all I could hear was his breathing.

I knew Dennis would be less than impressed with 'Henry's' non-performance so I scraped my shoe on the ground to try to stimulate the dog to bark, but still no response, other than his breathing getting heavier. I whispered "Speak" loud enough for the dog to hear several times, then suddenly the dog jumped over the wall and laid down beside me. Now we were both hiding from Dennis.

It may have been that 'Henry' had yet to meet a real villain, or that he knew me as John who rode in the Dog Van with him, or that he thought that what was good enough for me was good enough for him, and wasn't it a lot of fun being a police dog.

We repeated the exercise and this time 'Henry' got it right,

Dennis explained that 'Henry' did not want to join the police in the first place and had other plans which included parading down the Kings Road in Chelsea with a good looking lady on a posh lead, and a starring role at Crufts, not sodding about in a dirty old water works just to keep two scruffy old dog handlers in work.

Rabbi Fred

By BOB MARRION

In the world of canine enthusiasts it is often quoted that over a period of time a dog's character tends to adopt the characteristics of its owner, or handler (or is it vice versa?). In the case of police dog 'Fred' and handler, Frank Peters, this can be said to be true. Both rather small of stature and compactly built, plus a tad 'barbary' by nature, one always sensed that things were about to get 'interesting' when Frank began to remove his spectacles other than for the use for which they were intended.

I had known Frank from the time when he was a fresh faced, ever ready to please, young cadet at Arbour Square police station – until he became a dog handler alongside myself at Bow, with his never-to-be forgotten alter ego, 'Fred'.

'Fred' was not what one could call a particularly prepossessing or good looking animal, as previously stated he was rather small for a GSD, but sturdily built and with a rather indeterminate coat colour. His main attribute were his eyes, which could be best described as malevolent amber turning to orange when the thrill of the chase was in the air. Both dog and handler were eminently suited to each other, albeit making an extremely volatile mixture to be treated with care, best avoided by any other than fellow dog handlers considered part of the pack.

Throughout history, numerous earth shattering events came about by pure accident or coincidence. Whether Darwin's theories on evolution of the human species, or the workings of God (of whatever religious persuasion) brought about the anatomical make-up of a large dog, placing the 'sharp end' of nose, jaws and teeth just about the height of a male Homo Sapiens genitalia can only be surmised, or left to those ranking Chief Inspector and above whose sole purpose in life is to ponder such wonders. Such was the case bringing about the ingredients that have now passed into the annals of the CID and dog handlers, almost becoming a legend.

Many years have now gone by, and I cannot be sure how both

Frank and myself happened to be on night duty together, but I believe Frank and 'Fred' were of foot patrol, while I had been picked up by the 'H' Division 'Q' car with D/S Morecock and his crew. Now Lennie Morecock was a most enthusiastic and enlightened CID officer who saw the potential in police dogs and always tried to have me on board if it could be arranged when on night duty. He was also well liked by the uniform officers at Bow, unlike many CID officers at the time who considered us 'Wooden-tops', as something to be endured.

The quirky hand of fate decreed that DS Morecock and 'Fred' met in the doorway between the front office and the charge room. Now to 'Fred' a CID officer in plain clothes was not 'uniform' and thus not one of his pack. In a split second 'More' had become 'Less' with a virtual complete circumcision needing immediate hospital treatment. Len Morecock was the last person on earth to whom I would have wished such an embarrassing injury to happen, the embarrassment compounded by his surname. I could have thought of many more who had they suffered the administrations of 'Fred', I wouldn't have given a tinker's cuss. As a well known national newspaper columnist often says, 'You couldn't make it up'.

'Daddy's Smokums'
(or how I taught my dog to climb trees)
By BOB MARRION

Characters abound, along with many stories, associated with early dog handlers, many becoming almost legendary. Alf Peckham, Ernie Baxter, Tom Angus, 'Spike' Hughes to name but a very few of these 'golden oldies'. One of the leading characters who must rate 'Numero Uno' in the character stakes was the then Chief Instructor of the Training Establishment at Keston, Jim Morphy, who could put a name to every dog, but never remember a handlers name. We were all called 'Bill'.

When training my first dog, a trained handler and dog were attached to my class in an effort to remedy some doggie problem. The dog's name was 'Smokey', whose handler, if I remember correctly, was an older man than the rest of us trainees and a rather quiet, avuncular person.

It was not unusual that periodically the DTE was visited by various guests, or VIP's, to watch the various training exercises, most interest always being displayed in the 'blood sports' i.e. manwork. On one particular occasion, the then Commissioner, Sir Joseph Simpson, descended upon us. I believe he was the first Commissioner of Metropolitan Police to come through the ranks. He was a big man in all respects, a fine athlete and sportsman, universally liked by all. He commanded even more respect among we dog handlers when he played the part of a criminal for all our dogs in the manwork exercises.

I digress, however. On this particular day our 'guests' were members of a family of producers of a household name in the production of sausages and processed foods and, as was the case with such visits, accompanied by the inspector i/c admin and overall discipline etc, who, like all front men in all walks of life, could be considered more of the 'gentleman', ably suited for showing the great and the good around the establishment, unlike Jim who could be considered to be a little more 'earthy' and rougher round the edges.

The day in question was a quintessential English summer's day, clear blue sky, the nearby wood and countryside filled with birdsong, the Garden of England and the DTE in particular being at their very best, as the latter should have been, every inch having been cleaned from top to bottom as it was, in fact still is, when pre-warned visits are expected. Our entourage of visitors was escorted by our erstwhile inspector and Jim Morphy introduced the dogs, they being the 'stars', the handlers being considered lesser beings by dint of us being clothed in either blue overalls or boiler suits, supplemented by whatever else we could get hold of, plus our issue police caps, giving us the aspect of refugees from an establishment of correction, or some 'posh' borough dustmen and hardly worth consideration.

After a huddle between Jim and our host, it transpired that the latter had never been engaged in any manwork. Thus he wished to impress his visitors by acting the criminal in a 'seek' and probably be awarded first prize of a couple of pounds of sausages or pork pies for bravery in the field! 'Elf 'n Safety' being many more years in the future, along with the Dangerous Dogs Act, Jim most wisely decided that our inspector should be accompanied into the adjacent woods by his deputy, Bob Plumridge, whose knowledge of dogs and their behaviour was boundless. The trio set off into the woods with instructions that 'Smokey' be designated the starring role.

Now 'Smokey' was a rather unusual dog, both in coat colour and temperament; his coat was quite coarse, bordering on the long haired, best described as an ash grey in colour, hence, 'Smokey'. He also had a tendency not to bark on finding his quarry, but preferred an occasional 'nip' or pound of flesh instead. Another of his 'talents' was that he could jump, oh, how that dog could leap – Javier Sotomayor – or whoever holds the world high jump record, eat your heart out!

Now whether or not any of these rather important facts for the preservation of a person's well being were imparted, I know not, but suffice to say that three suitable trees were found and climbed, Jim and Bob apparently doing their best to emulate an Everest climber while the 'criminal' found a (what he thought was suitable) perch considerably lower, wishing to have a good clear view of a police dog in operation.

I now crave your indulgence and ask you to engage your imagination and picture if you can an idyllic summer's day only interrupted by the buzzing of bees, the distant sounds of passing traffic and the occasional passing aircraft overhead, a day when 'Ploughman's Lunch' plus a cool foaming pint, should have been the order of the day.

After the agreed time had lapsed, our instructor told 'Smokey's' handler to send in his dog. Most handlers treated their dogs more as an extension of their families and not just as an accessory to the job; 'Smokey' was treated more so by his handler. The result being that the dog was dubbed, 'Daddy's Smokums' by the rest of us.

To get back to the saga; off went 'Smokey' with great enthusiasm, disappearing into the depth of the wood. After what seemed an eternity, the great air of expectation was heightened by an increasingly agitated handler pacing up and down and heard to be muttering, with hands clasped in supplication to whoever answered his prayers, "Please let him find someone, or he'll come back and have me!"

An eternity was becoming an age when an almighty shriek rent the tranquil air, followed by yet another and then a loud fearful shout of 'Jim, Jim – Well don't sit there laughing. Get him off!' With this the class collapsed with laughter, followed by loud cheers when the trio emerged from the wood, our 'criminal' minus half a trouser leg (with fortunately no injury other than pride), followed by an ever thankful handler and triumphant 'Smokey'.

Jim and Bob Plumridge could hardly suppress their laughter. Later it transpired that the dog had found his 'criminal' without too much trouble, but true to fashion did not give tongue, balefully eyeing his victim and starting a rhythmical leaping gaining more height with each successive leap – six to eight feet seeming a mere bagatelle for old 'Smokey' whose perseverance eventually saw him getting his man – or at least his trouser leg!

Whatever happened behind closed doors of the inspector's office once our sausage bearing guests had departed was never known, other than our gallant inspector never again volunteered for any form of manwork, he just stuck to admin.

We never ever found out what happened to the sausages, but I have a good idea as Jim always greeted members of that particular class with a knowing smile and a wink along with his usual greeting of, 'Alright Bill, how's..........?' followed by the dogs name.

"Huh! Tales about police dogs, indeed!
I could tell a few tales about the handlers"

Old King Coal and the sack race

By BOB MARRION

Coal. That shiny black combustible rock upon which much of this country relied for heating, travel and industry, and of which children today know little or nothing. A fact brought home to me when my great grandson asked me "what was that shiny black stuff" he saw being shovelled into the firebox of a large model steam locomotive prior to a demonstration run.

As a result, memories came flooding back about those coal burning years. Of groping my way around a beat, day being turned into night by a thick yellow, sulphurous smog, lasting for days; of tripping up kerbs of drive-ins, hitherto never remembered as being there. Buses being guided by London Transport running inspectors holding flares, or coming off duty from a traffic point looking like a partially blacked-up Kentucky Minstrel. All the result of 'Old King Coal'.

My first police married quarters was the second in a terrace of thirteen police houses, divided between the sixth and seventh house by an alleyway leading to a rear service passage used for the delivery of utilities such as coal, etc. Our local coal merchant was also our local greengrocer whose shop was almost adjacent. An East Londoner of the old school with a heart as big as a pumpkin, respected by all and regarded with affection by all the kids from 'bogey mansions' who, on occasions, used to 'nick' a grape when not readily provided by his good self. He was, however, rather nervous when it came to the subject of dogs of all shapes and sizes and, at first, rather reticent to deliver coal to our quarters and to those of my next door neighbour, also a dog handler.

An agreement was reached and we were asked to secure our dogs indoors whenever coal was being delivered. We added a further cautionary condition that should the most unlikely occurrence of our coalman being greeted by a large, unfriendly police dog, he should immediately stand stock still, dropping his sack in front of him and face the dog – as if such a thing could ever happen. Could it?

It came to pass that we had an extra large delivery of the 'black diamonds' or 'nutty slack' at cheap summer prices shot into the back garden coal shed. Our intrepid coalman first ascertained that the dogs had been safely gathered in and were not lurking in their kennels. All was going swimmingly until my three year old daughter opened the back door to the garden to see if 'Pete' (for that was our coalman's name), had any grapes. As Pete was about to enter the garden, he was confronted by his worst nightmare, one rather large GSD hell-bent on protecting his territory and pack followed by a curly haired three year old asking for grapes!

Fear, or blind panic, makes people do strange things and terrified Pete forgot all previous instructions and was away on winged heels and halfway down the service passage before I realized what had happened. I flew out of the back door like a rocket. I was greeted by the sight of Pete breaking all records while carrying a one hundredweight sack of coal, plus the addition of one police dog on top of the sack and barking in Pete's right ear. This in turn motivated his legs to run even faster with no amount of shouted instructions from me telling him to stand still doing much good. I can only assume that with no visible arm or arms to hold, both being gainfully employed holding the large sack of coal on his back, the dog tried to get as close as possible to either appendage thinking this was a great new 'chase' exercise!

So we now had a hilarious scene of one panic stricken coalman complete with a one hundredweight sack of coal on his back, plus one furiously barking police dog on top of it almost nibbling Pete's ear, pursued by one three year old girl still asking whether he had any grapes, plus myself hard on their heels shouting "Stand still!". Fortunately, the gate between the alleyway and street was closed, forcing Pete to stop and follow my shouted instructions to drop the sack (he almost died of fright once he realized he had been carrying the dog) in front of him allowing me to bring the situation under control. Honeyed words, an angelic looking three year old – still asking for grapes – plus the promise of numerous bottles of

Guinness managed to placate our agitated coalman on a promise that I would make doubly sure that dog and kids were secure in future – or words to that effect – should I ever want more coal delivered!

My daughter is now fifty and we still have to hide the grapes when she visits.

How to make friends
By JEFF TERRY

It was an early turn and the good sergeant had arranged for Bob Sewell and I to attend a Jewish OAP club at Barkingside and give a talk about the dog section. At the allotted time we presented ourselves and received a warm welcome. After a short chat with the organizer and being forced to drink coffee and empty a plateful of biscuits he walked us onto a small stage and introduced us to an audience of about seventy people, all waiting with baited breath to hear our stories of heroic deeds! I volunteered to be the one showing the dog and Bob was left with the unenviable task of giving the talk. I knew he hated talking in public, but hey, one of us had to do it. I was full of admiration as he rattled on in his northern brogue, holding them in the palm of his hand as he informed them of the mystical art of training a dog He then threw in a couple of stories, turning us and the dogs into super-heroes.

Eventually, he paused for breath and asked the audience if they had any questions for him. Sitting in the front row was the most inoffensive, sweet looking woman in her mid seventies, the type you would willingly adopt as your grandmother. She raised a hand and waited for Bob to respond. 'Yes,' said Bob, expecting the usual gambit of 'Does he sleep in the house with you?' Oh, no! Her question was seriously challenging. 'I have a small Pekignese dog, officer. He is alright with me but whenever anybody else tries to pick him up he snaps at them. What do you think I should do?' Within the shortest time-span Bob stepped forward, placed his hands on his hips and looked down at the woman, replying 'I'd take the bloody dog to the vets and have it put down, Madam!' I took a sharp intake of breath, wondering as to which deck of which bus I was collecting fares when the said words were uttered. I needn't have worried, the audience rolled about with laughter like a group of Martians with their bellies full of mash.

I later remembered an old adage which was later translated into a song in the 50's:

"It's not what you say it's the way that you say it.

That's what gets results."

"Go away or my daddy will send these doggies"

Teresa Marrion, aged 4, with police dogs 'Lucky IV' and 'Liskah'. Teresa now serves in the Essex Force and has two daughters serving in the Metropolitan Force.

The Wedding

By OLIVE MARRION

We have all done it – forgotten our keys. One night, returning from a relative's wedding, Bob felt in his pockets, turned to me and said "have you got the front door keys?" Looking in my bag, I informed him that I did not. "Oh well" he said, "I'll have to climb through the kitchen window at the back." With my own Alsatian and police dog 'Liskah' inside we felt quite secure in leaving the kitchen fan light window open, which would give Bob easy access to the main window and thus gain entry. On putting his arm through the fan light he was met by two shapes of snarling fury, the sight of which scared me, as I had never seen this amount of aggression from a dog. No amount of soothing talk, followed by screams of expletives, calling his own dog all the names that he could think of, plus asking the animal whether or not he could recognise his working partner, who loved him, fed him, took him walkies, for rides in his nice police vehicle etc. Nope, he wasn't having any of it, as my dog was not going to let Bob in, neither was he. So, dressed in my nice wedding finery and hat, I was lifted up to try and soothe the savage beasts and did, much to Bob's chagrin (and I believe hurt pride.)

A bite between meals

By JEFF TERRY

It was a quiet night duty and Friday arrived without a sniff of a Form 12 (a report made as a result of good work by a Police Dog). I was posted to Juliet Zero dog van with Ted Berry and as midnight approached we resigned ourselves to being bombarded with stories from the neighbouring dog van of their incredible, lengthy and arduous searches and numerous arrests by their super dogs. Then came the call we were waiting for. "Any dog van assist with suspects decamped on Romford's section from a stolen vehicle...gone to ground in rear gardens. Meet Mr... at scene." I ripped the mike from its holder before the controller was halfway through his message, shouting back to MP that we were only two minutes away (a very slight exaggeration). Ted had already crashed through the gears and was in the process of pushing the accelerator through the foot well.

We arrived in a cloud of smoking rubber, both jumping from the van and haranguing the PC on scene for information on the suspect. He said it was best we speak to the friendly informant who was standing on the opposite pavement. The man informed us that the suspect had jumped a garden wall and was making his way across the rear gardens. Ted immediately took control, requesting the informant to remain at the scene and suggesting to me that I go with my dog to the alleyway at the rear of the gardens where I should wait and listen whilst he searched the gardens. I positioned myself as instructed, standing stock-still behind a garden wall, threatening my dog with double castration if he should utter a sound. Minutes expired before I heard a sound from within the garden I was standing behind. I tensed; grabbing my dog by his check-chain, ready to propel ninety pounds of canine fury at the miscreant should he oblige by attempting to flee the scene (after a challenge of course). Then nothing - not a peep, the night resuming its deathly vigil.

Eventually the suspense got the better of me. I levered myself up on top of the wall and peered into the garden, illuminated slightly by the light from within the house. Suddenly, Ted's exocet fur ball (Chips) arrived in padded glory, scrambling up the wooden panelled fence to my right and balancing himself on top like a thirty year sweat attempting the Force's fitness test for the first time. Ted always swore the dog was only eight years old? And then came the moment which shall be etched in my mind forever, a flashback not warranting embellishment, for clarity was crystallised in my unblinking eyes. It all happened in slow motion, six or possibly seven seconds, stretched out like a dream sequence in an action movie. Though only a few minutes had expired, our friendly informant had become anxious that the search should be progressed, not being acquainted with the timeless patience of the plodding dog handler. He had left the place where Ted had requested he remain and made his way into his home, the very home with the rear brick wall that I was perched on The noise I had heard was him unlocking his rear conservatory door, with the intention of entering his garden to assist the search, to guide us toward the suspect. I looked at him. I then looked at Ted's dog, still swaying on top of the fence like a pregnant trapeze artist. The informant adjusted his eyes to the gloomy light and then he too looked at the dog. I shouted 'No!' to the dog; 'Get inside!' to the informant; and 'Ted, put your dog down', to Ted (obviously) and then froze in unreasonable expectation that at least one of my requests would come to fruition. But we all know that true (dog-handling) life is not like that. It's more like 'Can I, shall I, oh heck...how do I get out of this fine mess?' So, Mr Informant, two steps outside the doorway, spots the dog. The dog spots Mr Informant. Ted spots neither because he was still two gardens away and besides that he couldn't hear my plaintive cry because his hearing was one decibel deficient due to years of wind-hammer pulsing through the open dog van window. Mr Informant made two steps towards his conservatory before Ted's dog latched onto his right buttock. His pained cry of anguish was totally washed out by cries of "Good boy...what you got son?" by a jubilant Ted who was typing his Form 12 in his head as he scaled the fence to join his dog and collect his prize.

Postscript: On realizing the small mistake Ted became very humble and apologetic, taking it upon himself to convey the informant to Oldchurch Hospital for the obligatory check-up and tetanus injection. I continued the search, which proved fruitless, and joined the pair in the casualty department some forty-five minutes later. I found them sitting on blue plastic chairs (which couldn't have been very comfortable for the informant) in a narrow corridor, awaiting the attendance of a hypodermic wielding nurse. I approached, with a correctly trained, serious look on my face, ready to offer my own sympathies to the aggrieved informant. I was stopped dead in my tracks by an eight foot by four foot advertising poster on the corridor wall directly opposite Ted and the informant. I blinked, cleared my eyes and read it again. You couldn't have made it up. No police canteen joker would have thought of a punch line so succinct as to place the proverbial cherry on the cake. There, in glorious Technicolor, was a picture of Snow White being followed by the Seven Dwarfs. A toothbrush was resting across their shoulders as they followed and sang the 'Hi Ho, Hi Ho, it's off to work we go!' jingle. Underneath, in bold print, was the caption - IF YOU FANCY A BITE BETWEEN MEALS (brush your teeth).

I nudged Ted and whispered 'Here, have you seen that poster'. His face was dead-pan (utter control, sheer professionalism!).

This story is true. ' I recall it of my own free will. I realise that anything said may be offered in print. The names of actual participants have not been changed expressly to protect the innocent. Long live the dogs!

A further 'Tail' from the crypt
By BOB MARRION

Available dogs from 'H' & 'G' Divisions, along with foot police, were detailed to gather at Tower Hamlets Cemetery one winters evening to search for property believed abandoned after a prior break in, the suspects having abandoned their loot within the cemetery.

Tower Hamlets Cemetery covered a fairly large area and, in parts, was very over grown. It was thought best to search the area in the late evening when there was less likelihood of anybody (other than the dead) occupying the location which at that time of the year was very unlikely. The cemetery dated back very many years, reputedly with the victims of the Great Plague being interred in mass graves; there were certainly mass graves for some of the first victims of the Blitz in the East End of London. So one could say that there was a certain ambience about the place during the hours of darkness and in winter particularly, with its fogs, heavy mists and moisture dripping from the leafless trees, the atmosphere could be downright 'Spooky'.

Starting out in a straight line with dogs intermittently spaced among the foot police, 'best laid plans of mice and men....' (to quote Robbie Burns) soon began to unravel. Groups and individuals became evermore isolated while negotiating the overgrown undergrowth, trees and numbers of hidden graves etc with only torches, plus the odd search lamp, any ambient street lighting filtering through the mist and trees began to get less illuminating. It was not long before I became isolated. Cursing and stumbling over hidden graves amongst this backdrop for a good old Hollywood 'B' horror movie and wishing unpleasant things for the 'brains' who organised this outing, I came across a mausoleum with gates open.

Believing this to be a likely place for miscreants to stash 'hooky' gear and if not, a good exercise for the dog, I released him to do a search – or that was the intention! The dog froze at the top of the steps leading down into the crypt. You can probably recall at some time or other, watching a cartoon animal character being a reluctant subject being put into a bath, kennel, strays van etc where they develop extra appendages to catch hold of every available toe hold to prevent this from happening – this proved to be a similar situation. Could I get my dog down into that dank hole? Could I hell!

On top of that, the batteries in my torch decided to go on the blink and through the light of its diminishing beam, I could just about make out the bottom of the stairs. With the dog's hackles up, ears and tail down and still no inclination to work that dank darkness, when under normal circumstances he would have gone through hell and high water, his courage never in question. As all my 'persuasive' efforts had failed and with an ever increasing sense of unease with visions of Count Dracula, Frankenstein's Monster, The Werewolf, zombies, ghoulies and other ghosties about to pounce, my sole object was to beat a hasty retreat. After all I was only paid to face the might of the criminal underworld and other ne'er do wells and not confront the combined forces of Hollywood's evil and horror.

So I did, closing the crypt gates behind me and whistling a merry little ditty, with my little legs getting ever faster, trying to keep up with the dog – well that's my excuse – making for the nearest available gap in the railings or exit.

That dogs, in fact most animals, have a sixth sense is not disputed, but what was down in that crypt that made my dog so reluctant to enter, has always intrigued me.

"Not much room left for the rest of you"
BMC mini van used as a dog van from early 1969. Two cages, one dog coming out from the vehicle rear, the other from behind the passenger.

Police rabbit

By BOB MARRION

Returning home from a visit to the barber prior to getting ready for a 'late-late' shift, I went into the garden to groom my dog. Shock! Horror! No dog. In its place was a large buck rabbit. Now I know I did not possess a rabbit prior to getting my hair cut. The only rabbit I had ever possessed was big and the only known man-eater, who attacked everything in sight, ending its days surrounded by pie-crust pastry! But that was many moons in the past.

Panic took hold when further searches did not reveal the dog, just the rabbit. Now I knew the difference between a dog and a rabbit, and still do – even in my dotage; the latter has shorter front legs, longer ears, a scut in place of a long tail and is considerably smaller. Had my workmate been morphed into a rabbit by some evil fairy as a practical joke? What would be my reception at the 'nick' if I presented myself for duty with a rabbit on the end of the leash? How long would it take me to pay for the loss of this precious and highly trained adjunct to police work? That is if I remained long enough in the police before being drummed out with ignominy. All these thoughts rushed through my head.

Interrogation of my four year old daughter revealed that although she loved 'Lucky', she fancied a change and had 'swapped' him for a police neighbour's daughter's rabbit, the mother of whom has sensibly secured the dog who, I must say, appeared to be completely content with his change of environment. Which says much about 'fierce' police dogs, who in the main, fitted into the family unit remarkable well as a pet, changing completely when it came to police work and could literally be turned 'on' and 'off' like an electric light switch.

Smarten up
By RAY PECKHAM

I shall resist telling the story about the night I fell out of a first floor landing bay window into the street below.

My dog followed on top of me. Duty Officer arrived on scene in time to see me untangling myself from my dog...Looked at this pile of dog and handler and says "Do your tunic up and put your bloody cap on".

Care of Police Survivors (COPS)

'Rebuilding Shattered Lives'

While realising the dangers of policing, no officer expects to die while on duty. When such a tragedy occurs, the surviving family endures emotions including denial, bewilderment, anger and depression. They also encounter many practical difficulties in respect of such a sudden loss. The police service does not have the resources, in most cases, to maintain support beyond the immediate aftermath of the death. This is where COPS comes in.

Care of Police Survivors is a charity dedicated to helping surviving families rebuild their lives after the trauma of an on duty death. It aims to provide the survivors with all the help they need to cope with such a tragedy and COPS ensures that they remain a part of the police family. The charity was founded in 2003 by retired detective Jim McNulty and Christine Fulton whose husband Lewis, an officer with Strathclyde Police, was murdered on duty in 1994 when their son was only seven months old. In 2008 Christine was awarded an MBE in recognition of her services to COPS.

Support is now provided to hundreds of bereaved police families. Sometimes an understanding listener is needed, sometimes more practical help is required and sometimes all that is needed is the reassurance that they are not alone and that the emotions they are feeling are normal. Events are held throughout the year which are especially suited to the different categories of survivors, mainly spouses, parents, children and siblings. On the last weekend of every July, COPS hosts a Survivor Weekend at the National Memorial Arboretum, Alrewas, Staffordshire where survivors come from all across the UK to spend time in the company of the only people who truly understand how they feel, other survivors. On the Sunday a Service of Remembrance is held when the survivors are joined by police and public to share in their loss and to remember the officers who have died.

Sadly, co-founder Jim McNulty died in 2004 but in his memory the Jim McNulty Memorial Fund was established which provides a block of ten driving lessons to survivor children on reaching the age of 17. As Jim was a former traffic officer and was passionate about cars and motorbikes it was felt that this was a fitting way to remember this remarkable man and something he would have fully approved of.

Like many small charities Care of Police Survivors relies on donations to continue its work and is grateful for the support it will receive from the sale of this book. Thank you and best wishes to all of its contributors and their canine colleagues.

COPS
PO Box 5685, Rugeley, WS15 9DN
Tel: 0844 893 2055, Fax: 0844 893 2056
Email: admin@ukcops.org
www.ukcops.org